TRIAL AND ERROR

A Comedy in Three Acts

by

KENNETH HO

SAMUEL FRENCH

LONDON
NEW YORK TORONTO SYDNEY HOLLYWOOD

ISBN 0 573 01460 4

MADE AND PRINTED IN GREAT BRITAIN BY
LATIMER TREND AND CO. LTD, PLYMOUTH
MADE IN ENGLAND

TRIAL AND ERROR

Presented by E. P. Clift and Linnit and Dunfee Ltd at The Vaudeville Theatre, London, on the 17th September 1953, with the following cast of characters:

(in the order of their appearance)

MRS O'CONNOR, the housekeeper	*Nan Munro*
DUDLEY, a visitor	*Derek Farr*
CLAUDE, the bridegroom	*Naunton Wayne*
ANDREA, the bride	*Constance Cummings*
GERTRUDE, the aunt	*Nora Nicholson*
BRIGGS, a girl reporter	*Patricia Heneghan*
RON, a press photographer	*Brian Smith*

The Play directed by ROY RICH
The Setting by RICHARD LAKE

SYNOPSIS OF SCENES

The action of the play passes in the living-room of a summer residence somewhere on the Sussex coast within easy reach of London, during a week in September

ACT I

Monday evening, after dinner

ACT II

Tuesday evening, before dinner

ACT III

SCENE 1　Wednesday afternoon, before tea
SCENE 2　Thursday afternoon, after lunch

Time—the present

To face page 1—Trial and Error

TRIAL AND ERROR

ACT I

SCENE—*The living-room of a summer residence somewhere on the Sussex coast within easy reach of London. A September Monday evening, after dinner.*

The room is gay, pleasant and modern. Illustrated opposite is the scene for the original production at the Vaudeville Theatre, but as the layout of this setting would be impracticable for most repertory companies and amateur societies, a modified version is shown on the Ground Plan at the end of the Play and stage directions have been adjusted accordingly. Up R there are spacious windows with a built-in seat. Immediately above this, french windows give on to a balustraded sun-deck outside, which leads off R to the beach and off L to the road. The windows and french windows together provide a wide view of sea and sky. There is a door back L leading to the kitchen and an open passage up L leads to the front door. Immediately below the passage a staircase leads up and off L to the bedrooms. A door down L opens into the library. In front of the window seat is a low table for meals. Armchairs stand down R and down L. There is a sideboard back C. A small table with a telephone on it stands L of the sideboard. There is a comfortable sofa at an angle LC with a low rectangular coffee table below it. Modern pictures hang on the wall up C and on the wall L, and there is a mirror on the wall down R. At night the room is lit by a standard lamp down R and table-lamps on the sideboard and telephone table. The sun-deck is furnished with an outdoor table and two chairs.

When the CURTAIN *rises, the stage is empty. It is dusk and the lights are lit. The french windows are open and the window curtains undrawn. A meal has been partly cleared from the table R. A bridal bouquet and Andrea's handbag are on the coffee table below the sofa. A knock is heard on the front door off. After a pause, the knock is repeated.* MRS O'CONNOR, *the housekeeper, enters from the kitchen. As she opens the kitchen door, dance music is heard coming from a radio receiver in the kitchen.* MRS O'CONNOR *is a spare, prim, bleak, middle-aged person of the "superior" type. She wears an overall and carries a tray. As she enters she speaks over her shoulder to someone in the kitchen.*

MRS O'CONNOR. Of course you don't mind. Why should you? *You* just sit and listen to your wireless. (*She crosses to the table R, her voice getting louder as the range increases*) *I'm* the one who has to do the work. *I'm* the one who's being kind, you know—not *her*. (*She stacks the dinner things on the tray*) All *she* does is to ask the people down here. Anyone can do *that*. I should be delighted to lend my house to people—if I had one—especially for a honeymoon. I shouldn't think it was *kind* of me, though—not if it was someone else who had to *do* everything. (*She picks up the cruet, napkins and table mats, moves to the sideboard, and puts them in the cupboard*) It's *doing* things for people that's *kind*, O'Connor, not getting others to do it. (*She crosses to the table* R) Especially with newlyweds. (*She picks up the tray and crosses to the kitchen door*) *They* don't know what *is* going on, half the time. Don't even appreciate what's being done for them.

> (MRS O'CONNOR *exits to the kitchen*)

(*Off*) Not that I've anything against *this* pair, mind you. You'd hardly know they *were* just married.

> (*The unintelligible rumble of a man's voice is heard, off.*
> MRS O'CONNOR *re-enters. She carries a crumb-tray and brush*)

(*She crosses to the table* R) I don't doubt it, O'Connor. I'm *sure* you wouldn't mind being in his shoes, knowing what you seem to think marriage is *for*. (*She brushes the crumbs from the table*) It doesn't surprise me in the least. The only thing that *is* surprising—is that you should ever have wanted to marry *me*—for I'm sure *I* don't inspire that sort of thing. (*She crosses to the sideboard, puts the crumb-tray and brush on it, picks up the bowl of flowers and places it on the table* R)

> (DUDLEY *enters the sun-deck from* L. *He is about thirty-five, well bred and charming, but there is something about him which fails to inspire confidence. He has a warm heart and a good temper, but doubtful standards. He wears a light raincoat over tweeds, and is bareheaded. He halts tentatively outside the french windows*)

(*She crosses to the sideboard*) You never called *me* a smasher, anyway. *That* I *do* know. (*She opens the sideboard cupboard, stoops and peers inside*) A simple English rose! That's what *I* was in *your* estimation. Not a . . .

> (DUDLEY *taps on the window jamb to attract Mrs O'Connor's attention*)

(*She straightens up. Startled*) Ooah! (*She turns to face Dudley*)

DUDLEY. I'm so sorry. I did try at the front, but . . . (*He breaks off*)

MRS O'CONNOR (*complainingly*) Well, all the bells are out of order, and you can't hear the knocker with *that*—(*she indicates the music*) going on. What is it you wanted?

DUDLEY. Do Mr and Mrs Merrilees live here?

MRS O'CONNOR. They're *staying* here, if that's what you mean. Got here this afternoon.

DUDLEY (*moving into the room*) Ah—then it *is* the house.

MRS O'CONNOR. They won't be receiving tonight, though.

DUDLEY (*confidently*) They'll see *me* all right. (*He wanders across to the sofa*)

Mrs O'Connor. They were only married this morning.

Dudley. I know. (*He grins disarmingly and sits on the sofa at the left end*)

Mrs O'Connor. They're out, anyway.

Dudley. When do you expect them back?

Mrs O'Connor. I've no idea. They're walking.

Dudley. *That* won't take 'em long, then—not if I know *her*. (*He takes an evening newspaper from his pocket, opens it and settles himself to read*)

Mrs O'Connor (*moving above the sofa; a little nonplussed*) Well, I've no wish to be rude, young man, but I'm afraid you can't stop there.

Dudley (*faintly surprised*) Can't I?

Mrs O'Connor. I have to go to bed.

Dudley (*surprised*) You don't sleep in here, do you?

Mrs O'Connor. Of course not. I can't *leave* you here—that's what I mean. I—I don't *know* you.

Dudley. Ah! I see your point. (*He folds the paper and replaces it in his pocket*)

Mrs O'Connor. It's nothing personal, I assure you.

Dudley (*rising*) My dear lady—you're so right. You'd be even less inclined to leave me here if you *did* know me. (*He smiles winningly and crosses up R*) I'll take a walk myself.

Mrs O'Connor (*softening somewhat*) What name shall I say—if I *am* still up?

Dudley. Mr Nightshade.

Mrs O'Connor. Oh. Well, I shouldn't be *too* long, if you *are* coming back.

Dudley. No. *They* won't be sitting up tonight, either, will they?

(Dudley *grins and exits on the sun-deck to* L)

Mrs O'Connor (*scandalized but quite thrilled*) *Well! What* a thing to say! (*She moves to the sideboard, picks up the crumb-tray, carries it to the coffee table and empties the ashtray. In a loud voice*) Did you hear any of that? A *man* came in. *Calling* on them, if you please. *Tonight.* Well, *I* don't . . .

(*The telephone rings*)

(*She mutters*) Oh, for heaven's sake. (*She moves to the telephone and lifts the receiver. Into the telephone*) Hullo? . . . Yes. . . . No, I'm afraid he's not . . . I've no idea, I . . .

(Claud *enters on the sun-deck from* R. *He is about forty, good-looking, honest, precise, respectable and kind. He is a trifle unimaginative but by no means lacking in wit, especially when annoyed, which is fairly often. He wears a suit of grey flannel*)

(*She sees Claud*) Oh, just a minute.

CLAUD (*crossing to the telephone; a little breathlessly*) Is that for me?

MRS O'CONNOR. Yes.

CLAUD. Ah! Thank you. (*He takes the receiver from Mrs O'Connor*)

(MRS O'CONNOR *exits to the kitchen. As she closes the door behind her the dance music ceases abruptly*)

(*Into the telephone*) Miss Winters? . . . (*He glances at his watch*) No, you're right on the nail. I cut it a bit fine getting back, that's all. Yes, on the—er—on the beach, as a matter of fact. Didn't notice the passage of time. You know how it is . . . (*He laughs self-consciously*) Oh, go on! You know you do. (*He laughs. Briskly*) Well, what happened about the Jones and Matherson thing? . . . Ah, that's all right, then. And Tilling Limited? . . . Good! We can leave that, too. Anything else come up? . . . Who? . . . What name? . . . Nightshade? . . . Haven't the least idea. Never heard of him.

(ANDREA *enters the sun-deck from* R. *She is thirty-two and very attractive. She is a woman of contrasts; easy-going, amiable and languid, yet with the temper of a squib. Maddeningly illogical—she is yet intuitively astute. She is exasperating and adorable. She wears her "going-away" dress and carries a long, trailing, ribbon-like bunch of seaweed. She stands just inside the french window, watching Claud*)

What did he want, then? . . . But didn't he say? . . . What? . . . Oh, I see. . . . Yes, most mysterious. Well, we shall soon find out, I expect. . . . Yes, I . . . (*He sees Andrea*) Just a minute. (*To Andrea*) What have you got there?

ANDREA (*holding up the seaweed; childishly pleased with it*) Seaweed.

CLAUD. Oh! (*He looks doubtfully at the seaweed. Into the telephone*) Sorry, I—just had to speak to my wife . . . (*He smirks*) Yes, it does seem strange, yes . . . Well, all right, Miss Winters, you'd better get to bed . . . No, I don't suppose we shall need any rocking, either. (*He catches Andrea's eye*)

(ANDREA, *in slight confusion, crosses and sits on the sofa, putting the seaweed beside her*)

(*Hurriedly*) I—I mean, er . . . Thank you. Good night. (*He replaces the receiver and moves above the sofa*) I say—do you think you ought to bring that in here? (*He leans over and picks up the seaweed*)

ANDREA. Why not?

CLAUD. Well, it is a borrowed house, isn't it?

ANDREA. It's perfectly clean. Some people eat it.

CLAUD. Some people eat horses—but you don't bring them indoors, do you?

ANDREA (*pleasantly sarcastic*) You're going to be far too clever for me, I can see that.

CLAUD. What shall I do with it, then?

ANDREA. Hang it up somewhere.

CLAUD. What for?

ANDREA. It also foretells the weather. Didn't you know?

CLAUD. Oh! (*He looks around, then crosses and hangs the seaweed on the picture down* L. *He then turns and stands smiling bashfully at Andrea*)

ANDREA (*beckoning*) Come.

(CLAUD *hesitates slightly, then, after a cautious glance towards the kitchen door, sits* L *of Andrea on the sofa.* ANDREA *leans back in the right corner of the sofa and pulls Claud to her so that he lies across her lap with his head to* R)

CLAUD (*warningly*) She's still about, you know.

ANDREA. Who is?

CLAUD. Mrs Whatsname.

ANDREA. Darling—we're married.

CLAUD (*uncomfortably*) Only this morning, though.

ANDREA (*squeezing him with impulsive enthusiasm*) Oh, I do think you're sweet.

CLAUD (*surprised*) What's sweet about that?

ANDREA. Have you ever paused to wonder why I should want to marry you?

CLAUD (*a little ruefully*) Yes—I must say I have.

ANDREA. It's for the very reason that you *are* like that.

CLAUD. Like what?

ANDREA. Afraid that Mrs Whatsname might come in. (*Ruminatively*) It's because you have such a sense of the *fitness* of things. It's because you tell the truth, and read *The Times*, and wear a bowler, and can't understand Picasso. It's because I'm sure you don't defraud the Inland Revenue or talk about women at the club. It's because you get all unhappy when I come indoors with seaweed. All those things. It's because you make such a *change*, I suppose.

CLAUD (*puzzled*) Change! From what?

ANDREA (*faintly surprised at the question*) My first husband, dear.

CLAUD (*not too pleased*) Oh! (*He draws away and sits up*)

ANDREA. He was nothing like that, you know—far from it. I got so that my yearning for respectability was almost morbid. So you've got him to thank for me, in a way.

CLAUD (*sourly*) I shall endeavour to keep that in mind.

ANDREA (*snuggling to him*) Why did you want to marry *me*?

CLAUD (*ill at ease*) I—I don't know. I'm not much given to that sort of analysis. I just couldn't resist you, I suppose.

ANDREA (*a little disturbed*) But you *must* have a better reason than that, dear—an experienced man like you. That's the mistake *I* made with *him*. Isn't there anything about me that you *admire?*

CLAUD. Yes, of course there is.

ANDREA. What, for instance?

CLAUD (*vaguely*) Well, I . . . Well—everything I *know* about you.

ANDREA. That can't be much. We only met three weeks ago. (*She sits up and looks at him*) Come to think of it—what *do* you know about me?

CLAUD (*harassed*) Well, I know you were a widow, of course. I know you're an orphan. I know you were brought up by an aunt. I know you've been living in France and—and so on and so forth.

ANDREA. That's not much of a reason for wanting to marry anyone, though, is it?

CLAUD. Well, of course it isn't. I don't mean that, I . . . (*He breaks off at a loss*)

ANDREA. You see, dear, what I *really* want to know is that it's not just physical.

CLAUD (*shocked*) Andrea!

ANDREA. Because that can be fatal, honestly. *I* know that only too well.

CLAUD (*affronted*) Do I *seem* the sort of man who . . . ?

ANDREA (*suddenly reassured*) No, dear, of course you don't. I'm just being silly. You're far too methodical. (*She puts her arm through his and leans her head on his shoulder*) No man who arranges for his secretary to ring him up on his honeymoon could *possibly* fail to have the most excellent reasons for getting married. (*She pauses. Conversationally*) Everything all right at the office?

CLAUD. Perfectly, thanks.

ANDREA (*with apparent enthusiasm*) Oh, *good!* (*She nestles to him*)

CLAUD (*suddenly remembering*) By the way . . .

ANDREA. Uh-huh?

CLAUD. D'you know a Mr Nightshade?

ANDREA. Not *now*, dear, no. Why?

CLAUD. Chap by that name got on to Miss Winters this afternoon. Wanted to contact you.

ANDREA. Me?

CLAUD. Yes—urgently.

ANDREA. What about?

CLAUD. Wouldn't say apparently. Doesn't it mean anything to you?

ANDREA. Not a thing.

CLAUD (*dismissing the subject*) Oh, well, she told him where to get you, so I expect you'll soon find out.

ANDREA (*sitting up; puzzled*) But who can the man be? Something to do with him, of course, but . . .

CLAUD (*interrupting*) Something to do with whom?

ANDREA. My first husband, dear.

CLAUD (*blankly*) Why?

ANDREA. Well, his name was Nightshade.

CLAUD (*looking at her; perplexed*) Nightshade?

ANDREA. Yes.

CLAUD. But how can that be?

ANDREA. Why shouldn't it?

CLAUD. You were Mrs St John Willoughby.

ANDREA. I changed my name, Claud—by deed poll. Didn't I tell you?

CLAUD. No.

ANDREA (*put out*) Oh, I *am* sorry. Oh, *Claud*. I wouldn't have had that happen for worlds, because, if there's one thing I'm determined upon *this* time, it's to start with no shadow of misunderstanding on either side.

CLAUD. I can't see that it matters much what your name was.

ANDREA. But it isn't that. It's a matter of trust.

CLAUD. It was only an oversight, anyway.

ANDREA (*gloomily*) I know. I had a terrible time with Dudley on account of oversights.

CLAUD (*irritably*) Who's Dudley?

ANDREA. My first husband, dear.

CLAUD. I thought you said his name was Roderick.

ANDREA. So it was. (*She idly takes up the bouquet*) I used to call him Dudley, though, because I thought it went better with Nightshade.

(CLAUD, *looking deeply perplexed, rises and stands* L *of the sofa*)

CLAUD (*suddenly pointing at Andrea*) Oh, yes! (*He laughs, then crosses above the sofa to the french windows and gazes out*) Whatever possessed you to marry such a chap, though?

ANDREA. I told you. I couldn't resist him. I knew perfectly well he was only after my money, but—(*with a touch of nostalgia*) oh, he had such charm.

(CLAUD *glances coldly at Andrea*)

I don't think I ever met anyone who . . .

(CLAUD, *struck by a sudden thought, turns abruptly*)

CLAUD (*interrupting*) But, look here, Andrea——

ANDREA. Yes?

CLAUD (*moving down* C) —I thought you hadn't got any money.

ANDREA (*hanging her head and fiddling with the ribbon of the bouquet*) Yes—I know I told you that.

CLAUD. Then how could he have . . . ?

ANDREA (*rising*) Darling! (*She crosses swiftly to* L *of Claud and stands close to him, looking deeply contrite)* I lied to you—I've got quite a lot.

CLAUD. You have?

ANDREA. My aunt left it to me—the one who brought me up.

CLAUD *(bewildered)* What on earth's the point of lying about that?

ANDREA. Well, you see . . . *(She breaks off)*

CLAUD. Yes?

ANDREA. I wanted so much to be sure that—you weren't doing —what he did.

CLAUD. What, marrying you for your . . . ? *And*rea! *(He turns angrily away and moves down* R)

ANDREA *(crossing to* L *of Claud)* I didn't know what you were like then. I hardly knew you.

CLAUD *(shocked)* I dare say you didn't, but even so . . .

ANDREA *(taking his arm)* Don't be hurt, dear, please.

(CLAUD *turns his head away)*

It's only right to profit from past mistakes. You must see that.

CLAUD. Well, having duly profited, I suggest that we now forget the past—and everything in it.

ANDREA *(meekly)* Certainly, dear, if you wish.

CLAUD. And turn our attention to the future, for a change.

ANDREA. Of course. *(She turns his face towards her)* What's wrong with the present, though—*(she holds up her face provocatively)* in the meantime?

(CLAUD *seems momentarily to resist, then after a precautionary look towards the kitchen door, takes Andrea in his arms and kisses her)*

CLAUD *(taking her by the hand)* Come and sit down.

(CLAUD *strides to the sofa, dragging* ANDREA *after him.* ANDREA *throws her bouquet on to the coffee table.* CLAUD *sits on the sofa at the left end, and draws* ANDREA *down after him so that she now reclines across his lap)*

ANDREA. We're going to be so happy.

(They kiss, but in the middle of the embrace, CLAUD *seems to lose interest. His face comes up a little, wearing a thoughtful look)*

(Faintly alarmed) What's the matter?

CLAUD *(with his face still very close to hers)* Look—I don't want to pry into your affairs, of course, but *why* did you change your name?

ANDREA *(surprised at the question)* Well, wouldn't you have done —in similar circumstances?

CLAUD *(looking blank)* What circumstances?

ANDREA *(sitting up and staring at him)* You—you can't mean that you don't know what I'm referring to?

Claud. Well, I don't, I can assure you.

Andrea (*rising and crossing to* R; *suddenly agitated*) But it isn't possible. (*She turns and faces him*) Don't you ever read the papers? *Heaven knows* they made enough fuss about it.

Claud (*rising; with the air of one who has taken enough*) Andrea—if you're trying to tell me that there was some sort of a scandal—honestly, I think I'd rather not . . . (*He breaks off and moves down* L)

Andrea. *Scandal!* My dear, you don't know what you're saying. Why do you think I went to live in France?

Claud. I've no idea why anyone should live in France—except the French.

Andrea (*moving up* C) But, this is awful, Claud. (*She turns*) I don't know what to say. I took it that you *knew*. (*She moves down* C) The very fact that you never mentioned it made me think that. I thought you were being delicate about it.

Claud. How could I mention something that I didn't know of?

Andrea. Oh, I see that now, but I thought everyone knew. Why, good gracious me, I'm pointed out to American tourists in the streets of Cannes.

Claud. What as?

Andrea (*evasively*) Well—as the—as the woman who changed her name.

Claud (*crossing to* L *of Andrea*) But why, Andrea?

Andrea (*avoiding his eye*) Because—well, because of the things that came out in court.

Claud. Ah! "*Court*"*!* I see. So that's another lie, is it?

Andrea (*indignantly*) What is?

Claud. I thought you were supposed to be a widow.

Andrea (*quite pained*) Claud—you don't think it was a *divorce* court, do you?

Claud. Wasn't it?

Andrea (*shocked*) Good heavens, no.

Claud. Oh!

Andrea. I *am* a widow—or rather, I was—until this morning. He fell off a liner.

Claud. Who did?

Andrea. Dudley. In the middle of the sea. (*She turns away*)

Claud. I'm sorry. I didn't realize. It was a Court of Enquiry?

(Andrea *clears her throat and looks at her feet*)

Is that what you mean?

Andrea (*innocently*) What, dear?

Claud. It was a Coroner's Court?

Andrea (*looking uncomfortable*) Well, not exactly, no. You see—I was supposed to have *pushed* him off the liner.

Claud (*incredulously*) You were supposed to have pushed him off the liner?

ANDREA (*airily*) Yes.

CLAUD. Deliberately?

ANDREA. Oh, yes.

CLAUD (*staggered*) You—you don't mean . . . You can't mean that—that it was a Criminal Court?

ANDREA. Old Bailey!

CLAUD (*staring at her*) You were accused of . . . ? (*He breaks off*)

ANDREA. Tried for it.

CLAUD. Murder?

ANDREA (*a little impatiently*) Well, of course, Claud.

CLAUD (*horrified*) Andrea! (*He turns away down* LC)

ANDREA (*a little sulkily*) I got off.

CLAUD (*turning; with sudden violence*) Well, of course you got off. I can see that.

ANDREA (*in slightly hurt tones*) There's no sense in getting huffy about it, dear. After all, it is over and done with. (*She moves and sits on the downstage end of the window seat*) It wasn't my fault, anyway.

CLAUD (*crossing to her*) Whose fault was it, then?

ANDREA. Phoebe Hogg's.

CLAUD. Who the hell's Phoebe Hogg?

ANDREA. Oh, some fool of a girl on the ship. (*Resentfully*) There wouldn't have been any fuss at all if it hadn't been for her.

CLAUD. What did *she* do?

ANDREA. Said she saw me, that's all.

CLAUD. Saw you what?

ANDREA (*her tone suggesting that Claud is being very obtuse*) Push Dudley *in*, Claud.

CLAUD (*clapping his hand to his brow*) This is frightful! (*He crosses down* C)

ANDREA (*aggrieved*) I can't see what's so frightful about it. He was an awfully bad man, anyway.

CLAUD (*turning and staring at her*) Do you mean by that, that there was a miscarriage of justice—that you *shouldn't* have got off?

ANDREA (*indignantly*) Of course I don't. I had every right to.

CLAUD (*relaxing with relief*) Oh! (*He crosses to the armchair down* R *and sits*)

ANDREA. There wasn't enough evidence.

CLAUD. What!

ANDREA. Even the judge admitted that—and he was on the other side.

(CLAUD *seems to give up. With a gesture of defeat, he abandons himself to a sort of stunned gloom*)

(*She regards Claud with compassion for a moment, then rises and moves to* L *of him. Kindly*) Darling—this is worrying for you, I can see that. Wouldn't it be better if you let me tell you about it?

CLAUD (*sarcastically*) Perhaps it would.

(ANDREA *sits on the floor at Claud's feet*)

ANDREA. Well, you see—Dudley and I were coming back from Cape Town where we'd been to see some friends—and the ship was somewhere off that lump—you know—that sticks out on the left-hand side of Africa. (*She pauses and looks up at him*)

(CLAUD *nods*)

Well, it was a very hot night, and also there had been a bit of a party. Heaven knows what *he'd* had, but I'd had two glasses of champagne and a green Chartreuse. So I . . . (*She breaks off. Thoughtfully*) Or was it Crème de Menthe?

CLAUD (*wearily*) Does it matter?

ANDREA. Yes, dear, it does matter. You don't know what false-hood can do to a marriage. I do. He was a shocking liar.

CLAUD. I see. I'm sorry.

ANDREA (*thoughtfully*) I think it was green Chartreuse.

CLAUD. Right.

ANDREA. So I got Dudley to take me up on to the boat deck for some fresh air, d'you see? And when we were up there, a scarf I was wearing blew off and caught under one of the boats, and Dudley very kindly climbed over the railings to get it for me. (*She pauses*)

CLAUD. Well?

ANDREA. Well, now—according to the prosecution—that's where I saw my opportunity—see? They said I leaned over the railings and pushed him.

CLAUD (*sitting forward to question her*) That's what the prosecution said?

ANDREA. Yes.

CLAUD. And what about the defence?

ANDREA. My counsel you mean? Old Smithers?

CLAUD. Yes. What did he say?

ANDREA (*giggling*) I couldn't make out what he was talking about half the time.

CLAUD (*persevering patiently*) Look! Did he put you in the witness-box?

ANDREA. Yes.

CLAUD. Well, what did you say yourself?

ANDREA. About what?

CLAUD (*with iron control*) In answer to the charge that you leaned over the railings and pushed him.

ANDREA. Oh, I just said I was trying to get him back.

CLAUD. Andrea—how did the prosecution know that you were doing anything at all?

ANDREA. Ah, that's where the girl comes in.

CLAUD. The one who was supposed to have seen it?

ANDREA. Yes.

CLAUD. And she thought you were pushing—*not* pulling?

ANDREA. She was *sure* I was pushing.

CLAUD. But it was dark. How could she be sure?

ÁNDREA. Oh, she could see all right. There was such a lovely moon.

CLAUD. Then how were you able to show that she was wrong?

ANDREA. I wasn't. It was her word against mine, that's all.

CLAUD (*hopefully*) Well, it was yours that they believed, anyway.

ANDREA. Do you know—I don't think anyone believed a word I said from start to finish.

CLAUD (*getting quite frantic*) But, Andrea, they *must* have done.

ANDREA. Why?

CLAUD. You were acquitted.

ANDREA. Ah, but that wasn't so much a matter of believing me as disbelieving the girl. You see, she'd been having a party, too.

CLAUD. You mean they couldn't rely on her evidence?

ANDREA. That's it, exactly. (*She rises, yawns and crosses to* C) Well—it was nasty while it lasted—but all's well that ends well, and . . .

CLAUD (*rising in dismay; interrupting*) But that's not *all*? (*He crosses to* R *of her*) You're not going to leave it at that?

ANDREA. It's all that mattered, dear. (*She picks up her handbag from the coffee-table and searches vaguely in it*) There were one or two people who came in and said that Dudley had seduced their wives—you know—to show motive—and a charwoman who testified that she'd seen me hit him with a piece of Crown Derby, which was a lie because it was Spode—(*she closes her handbag*) but nothing of importance. It all really centred round the . . .

CLAUD (*interrupting*) Andrea—(*he crosses and stands above the sofa*) don't you realize that what I want to know is not whether you got off; it's not even *how* you got off—it's whether you *did* it?

ANDREA (*putting her handbag on the coffee table*) How do you mean? (*She sits on the sofa at the right end*)

CLAUD (*moving to* L *of the sofa*) Whether you did push him in.

ANDREA. Didn't I say?

CLAUD. No, you didn't say.

ANDREA. Oh! (*In faint surprise*) And you want me to?

CLAUD. Well, of course I want you to.

ANDREA (*blankly*) Why?

CLAUD. What do you mean, "why"?

ANDREA. I should have thought you'd take it for granted that I didn't.

CLAUD (*uncomfortably*) Well, I do, but . . .

ANDREA. Without having to be told. D'you think I should be likely to do a thing like that?

CLAUD. No, but . . .

ANDREA. Then, why ask?

CLAUD. Well . . .

ANDREA. Don't you trust me?

CLAUD. Yes, of course I trust you.

ANDREA. Then, I'm sorry, dear—but I don't understand.

CLAUD (*with a defeated air*) All right. Forget it. (*He moves to the armchair down* L *and sits*)

ANDREA. I'll tell you with pleasure if you want me to, of course, but . . .

CLAUD (*interrupting; loudly*) The question's withdrawn. (*He folds his arms and turns away*)

ANDREA. Thank you, darling.

CLAUD. And I'm sorry.

ANDREA (*smiling indulgently*) There's no need to be sorry. You spoke without thinking, that's all. (*Briskly*) Now! Let's talk about something not so . . .

CLAUD (*interrupting*) I don't want to talk about anything, if you don't mind.

(ANDREA, *dismayed, rises, crosses to Claud, goes down on her knees and puts her arms about him*)

ANDREA. Darling—don't be cross. I know it was wrong of me not to make sure that you knew about all this before, but—please don't be cross.

(CLAUD *does not reply*)

Please, Claud. It worries me when you behave like this. It's just the way Dudley started.

CLAUD (*bitterly*) Did you forget to tell him something, then?

ANDREA (*sitting back on her heels; a little self-consciously*) As a matter of fact, I did.

CLAUD (*sarcastically*) There wasn't another husband who fell off a liner, was there, before him?

ANDREA (*ignoring his ill-temper*) I neglected to mention that my aunt would be living with us, that's all.

CLAUD (*turning to her*) Oh! Is she going to live with us, too?

ANDREA. She's dead, dear.

CLAUD. You're sure of that?

ANDREA (*laughingly*) Of course I'm sure. (*She rises and moves below the coffee table*) I nursed her in her last illness.

CLAUD. Is that the one who left you the money?

ANDREA (*brightly*) That's right. (*She takes up the bouquet*)

CLAUD. I thought you said he married you for your money?

ANDREA. So he did.

CLAUD. But how could he have done if your aunt was still alive when he married you?

ANDREA (*idly examining the flowers*) Well, he could see how

B

decrepit she was, Claud. Anyone could. That's what I mean. It was so silly of him to make such a fuss. She couldn't hope to be with us for long, poor pet. Though, oddly enough, it wasn't old age that she died of at all, in the end.

(CLAUD *seems suddenly gripped by a horrid suspicion*)

CLAUD (*stiffening*) What did she die of, Andrea?

(ANDREA *buries her nose in the flowers for a moment, then looks up*)

ANDREA. Botulism.
CLAUD. What the hell's botulism?
ANDREA (*turning to him; plaintively*) Claud—we don't want to talk about things like that. This is our wedding night.
CLAUD (*with a sort of bitter surprise*) Good God! So it is. (*He turns away, morosely hunched in his chair*)

(ANDREA *stands a moment looking a little forlornly at Claud's uncompromising back view*)

ANDREA (*sighing*) Well—I'm going to bed, anyway.

(ANDREA *crosses above the sofa and exits up the stairs.* CLAUD *rises and crosses in aimless agitation to* R)

CLAUD (*muttering worriedly*) Botulism! Botulism!

(MRS O'CONNOR *enters from the kitchen. As she opens the kitchen door the dance music is heard coming from the radio receiver in the kitchen*)

MRS O'CONNOR. Oh, I forgot to tell you. A gentleman called. Wanted to . . .
CLAUD (*interrupting*) Mrs O'Connor, is there a dictionary in the house?
MRS O'CONNOR (*indicating the door down* L) Well, that's the library. I don't know whether . . .

(DUDLEY *enters on the sun-deck from* L)

CLAUD (*interrupting*) Ah! (*He crosses to the door down* L) Thank you.
DUDLEY (*calling*) I say!

(CLAUD *stops and turns in surprise*)

MRS O'CONNOR. Ah!

(MRS O'CONNOR *turns and exits into the kitchen. As she closes the door behind her the dance music ceases abruptly*)

DUDLEY (*advancing a little into the room*) I'm terribly sorry to come in like this. I'm sure it's not convenient, but . . . (*He breaks off*) You *are* Mr Merrilees, I take it?
CLAUD. What is it you want?

DUDLEY (*crossing to* R *of the sofa*) Well—that's a thing I think I'd better lead up to a little. (*He takes off his coat*) You see, what I have to tell you . . .

CLAUD (*interrupting*) Look—I'm awfully sorry, my friend; I don't know who you are or what you're doing here, but it's late, and I want to go to bed.

DUDLEY (*meaningly*) I can well understand that you do—but that, unfortunately, is the very thing that I'm here to prevent. (*He throws his coat over the back of the sofa*)

CLAUD. What the devil do you mean?

DUDLEY (*regretfully*) I had intended—in common humanity— to break it gently. But I perceive that you are not a man with whom the indirect approach is possible. (*He fixes Claud with his eye*) I—am Roderick Nightshade, Mr Merrilees.

CLAUD. Oh, you're the man who called at my office?

DUDLEY. That is so.

CLAUD. Well, what's it all . . . ? Did you say *Roderick* Nightshade?

DUDLEY. I did.

CLAUD (*staring at him*) But—but that was the name of my wife's first husband.

DUDLEY. That *is* the name of your wife's first husband.

CLAUD (*incredulously*) You don't mean . . . ? You're not imply-ing . . . ? (*He breaks off*)

DUDLEY (*with real regret*) I can't tell you how sorry I am.

CLAUD (*crossing hurriedly to Dudley; delightedly*) But this is won-derful! (*He holds out his hand*)

DUDLEY (*astonished*) Huh?

CLAUD (*seizing Dudley's hand and wringing it*) I'm overjoyed— delighted. You—you don't know what a relief it is. I couldn't be more pleased.

DUDLEY (*mystified*) But, look . . .

CLAUD (*interrupting*) And Andrea. Just think what it will mean to her. (*He drops Dudley's hand and crosses to the staircase*) I must tell her. I must tell her at once.

DUDLEY. But just a minute.

CLAUD (*stopping and turning*) Yes?

DUDLEY (*looking bemused*) I don't quite follow this. Why should you be pleased to see me?

CLAUD (*crossing to* L *of Dudley; in some surprise*) Why—your mere presence here, my dear fellow. The very fact that you're *alive*. Surely you must realize what a terrible shadow it lifts from my married life?

DUDLEY. I should have thought it meant you hadn't *got* a married life.

CLAUD. What? (*The elation drains from his face*)

DUDLEY. Well . . . (*He breaks off regretfully*)

CLAUD. You don't mean that you still regard yourself as married to Andrea?

DUDLEY. Nothing's happened to unmarry us—has it?

CLAUD (*looking completely stunned*) No, I . . . Good heavens!

DUDLEY (*taking Claud's arm and leading him to the sofa; kindly*) Look! You sit down, old chap, and let me get you a drink.

(CLAUD *sinks on to the sofa.* DUDLEY *moves to the sideboard and pours two neat whiskies*)

CLAUD (*after a dazed pause*) But—this morning. What we went through together this morning. Was it—meaningless?

DUDLEY (*reluctantly*) Well—not so much meaningless, perhaps, as—bigamous.

CLAUD (*moaningly*) Oh no! That's too much!

DUDLEY (*picking up the drinks and moving to* R *of the sofa*) Don't see how it can be anything else. (*He hands a glass to Claud*)

CLAUD (*almost snatching the glass; in sudden anger*) For God's sake, then, why did you leave it until now?

DUDLEY. I didn't know where she was. Couldn't find her. (*He moves above the sofa, takes a newspaper from the pocket of his coat, then moves to* L *of the sofa*) I shouldn't know now, if it hadn't been for this. (*He puts his glass on the coffee table, then reads from the paper*) "Mr Claud Merrilees, the architect, and Mrs Andrea St John Willoughby, leaving Caxton Hall after their marriage this morning." (*He hands the paper to Claud*) There you are. Lunch Edition. First I knew of it. (*He picks up his drink, moves to the armchair down* L *and sits*)

(CLAUD *puts his glass on the coffee table, takes his spectacles from his pocket, puts them on and looks gloomily at the picture in the paper*)

I got your office from the telephone directory—found out where you'd gone—borrowed a car from a friend—and came down. Didn't waste much time. (*He suddenly looks puzzled*) By the way——

CLAUD. Well? (*He replaces his spectacles in his pocket*)

DUDLEY. —has she married somebody else in the meantime, or what?

CLAUD (*startled*) Uh? Not that I know of. Why?

DUDLEY. Then why the "Mrs St John Willoughby"?

CLAUD (*relaxing*) Oh, that. She changed her name, that's all.

DUDLEY (*perplexed*) Changed it! What for?

CLAUD (*rising and throwing the newspaper on the coffee table; irritably*) Oh, use your brain, man, for heaven's sake. (*He moves up* R)

(ANDREA *enters down the stairs*)

ANDREA (*as she enters*) Forgot to put the car away. (*She turns towards the passage up* L) Really, dear, you must learn to drive. (*She glances at Claud, sees his glum look, turns and crosses towards him*) Claud—you're not still fussing about . . .

(DUDLEY *slowly rises*)

(*She glances at Dudley, continues on a few steps, then stops in her tracks and turns to stare at him. For a moment she remains thus, frozen with astonishment*) No—it can't be!

DUDLEY (*smiling regretfully*) It is, you know. (*He puts his drink on the coffee table*)

ANDREA (*moving to* R *of the sofa; dazed*) We—we thought you were dead.

DUDLEY (*moving below the coffee table; with a glance at Claud*) So I gather.

ANDREA (*suddenly running to Dudley*) Oh, but how lovely. (*She locks him in a fervent embrace*) I—I can't believe it. (*She kisses him heartily then turns to Claud*) It's Dudley, dear—alive. (*To Dudley*) Oh, but you've met my husband.

DUDLEY⎱ (*together*) ⎰Yes. (*He inclines his head to Claud*)
CLAUD⎰   ⎱How d'you do? (*He bows slightly*)

ANDREA (*to Dudley*) We were only married this morning—and now you. (*She squeezes his arm*) Oh, darling, this makes my day complete.

(*Neither man seems quite equal to the situation.* DUDLEY *is a little embarrassed.* CLAUD *looks on unbelievingly*)

DUDLEY. Well, I'm—glad you're pleased to see me, Andrea.

ANDREA. How can you say such a thing? It's like another wedding present. (*She draws Dudley towards the sofa*) Here, come and sit down. Get him a drink, Claud. (*She sees the glasses on the coffee table*) Oh—you have. (*She plants* DUDLEY *on to the sofa, hands him his drink, and then sits* R *of him*) Oh, this *is* nice.

DUDLEY. Actually I felt a bit awkward—barging in at a time like this.

ANDREA. Awkward? Why?

DUDLEY. Well, I knew you'd just got married, and . . .

ANDREA (*interrupting*) Why didn't you come to the wedding?

DUDLEY (*picking up the newspaper*) I didn't know until it was over. (*He indicates the picture*)

ANDREA (*taking the newspaper; interestedly*) Oh—a picture! (*She studies the picture. To Claud*) What a pity you were making such a face, dear. (*She puts the newspaper on the coffee table. To Dudley*) But where have you *been* all this time?

DUDLEY (*something in his manner becoming subtly evasive*) It's a bit of a long story, really.

ANDREA (*innocently*) Oh, we're in no hurry to go to bed—(*to Claud*) are we?

(CLAUD *shakes his head in a dazed sort of way, shrugs slightly, then moves to the left end of the window seat and sits*)

(*To Dudley*) And how did you manage it? I mean, the last I saw of you, you seemed to be going down for the third time.

DUDLEY. Somebody heaved a lifebuoy after me. I hung on to that.

ANDREA. The captain wasted hours looking for you, dear.

DUDLEY. I know.

ANDREA. He was furious.

DUDLEY (*plaintively*) I couldn't make myself heard.

ANDREA. How long did you have to hang on to the lifebuoy, then?

DUDLEY (*resentfully*) Until about half-way through the next day.

(ANDREA *makes a sympathetic noise*)

Then I was picked up by some native fishermen—that's about all there is to it, really. (*He does not seem anxious to pursue the subject*)

ANDREA. But where have you been ever since?

DUDLEY (*vaguely*) Out there.

ANDREA. In Africa?

DUDLEY. Yes.

ANDREA. Why didn't you let me know, dear?

DUDLEY (*hesitantly*) I—I'd lost my memory, Andrea.

ANDREA. You what?

DUDLEY (*with apparent effort*) You see—it had all been rather a shock. I—I was really quite ill. Even now I . . . (*He breaks off, puts his glass on the coffee table, and passes a shaky hand across his brow. One feels that he is acting*)

ANDREA (*in deep sympathy*) Oh—poor darling.

CLAUD (*rather aggressively*) Hadn't you anything in your pockets to identify you?

DUDLEY (*pitifully*) Nothing. I—just didn't know who I was.

ANDREA. Perhaps you'd rather not talk about it, dear?

DUDLEY (*gratefully*) Well, if you don't mind, I . . .

CLAUD. How long did this go on, then—not knowing who you were?

DUDLEY. Until quite recently.

ANDREA. Nearly a year?

DUDLEY. Yes. As soon as I remembered, of course, I came back for you.

ANDREA (*understandingly*) Of course.

CLAUD. He couldn't find you, though—or that's what he says.

ANDREA. Well, naturally, Claud. I'd changed my name and gone to live in France.

DUDLEY (*puzzled*) Yes—what was the idea of that?

ANDREA. What?

DUDLEY. Calling yourself Mrs St John Willoughby.

ANDREA (*blankly*) I liked the sound of it, that's all. I mean—if you *have* got to change your name, you might as well pick one you like.

DUDLEY. But, that's what I mean. Why change it at all?

ANDREA. Well, because . . .

CLAUD (*suddenly rising and moving down* R) Well, I'm sorry, but I don't believe a word of it.

ANDREA. What?

CLAUD. All this nonsense about amnesia. He could easily have found out who he was through the name of the ship on the lifebuoy for one thing—if he'd wanted to.

ANDREA. Well, you don't think *I* believe it, do you?

CLAUD (*surprised*) Don't you?

ANDREA. My dear Claud, nobody ever believes Dudley.

DUDLEY (*picking up his drink; quite unabashed*) I must say I hadn't thought of that, though—about the lifebuoy.

ANDREA (*to Claud*) You see? He hardly expects to be believed. (*Reprovingly*) But I don't think *you* know him well enough, yet, to try and trip him up like that.

CLAUD (*moving to the french windows*) Well, I devoutly hope I shall never know him any better. (*He gazes out of the window*)

ANDREA (*rising and crossing to* L *of Claud*) Claud dear, I can't think why you're adopting this attitude to Dudley. He hasn't done anything to you. (*She glances at Dudley*)

(DUDLEY *avoids Andrea's eye*)

(*Suspiciously*) Or has he?

CLAUD (*turning to Andrea*) He's only turned up on my wedding night and claimed my wife as his, that's all.

ANDREA (*at first uncomprehendingly*) Your wife? Oh, me, you mean?

CLAUD. Yes—you.

ANDREA (*turning and looking at Dudley*) But he's only joking.

CLAUD. Ask him.

DUDLEY (*uncomfortably*) I've told him how sorry I am. I don't know what more I can do.

ANDREA (*crossing to* R *of the sofa; incredulously*) Do you mean that you *are* claiming me?

DUDLEY (*with a note of defiance*) I don't have to. You—are my wife, and I'd rather like to have you back, that's all.

ANDREA (*astounded*) What on earth are you talking about, Dudley? And, for heaven's sake, what do you want me back for? You never appreciated me when you had me.

(DUDLEY, *his manner suddenly grave, puts his glass on the coffee table, rises and turns away* L *before replying*)

DUDLEY (*acting*) No—I didn't. God knows I didn't. It wasn't until I—couldn't find you, Andrea—until I began to think that I might never see you again, that—I realized what had gone out of my life.

ANDREA. What had, dear?

DUDLEY. Something—healing.

CLAUD (*muttering*) Healing, my foot!

DUDLEY (*apparently deeply moved*) I just found that I—couldn't get on without you, Andrea, that's all.

CLAUD. Couldn't get on without her money, more like it.

ANDREA (*wearily*) Claud dear, please don't keep on pointing out the obvious. I'm trying to find out why he thinks he's my husband. (*To Dudley*) *Have* you a reason?

DUDLEY. Only that I married you first.

ANDREA (*relieved*) Oh, well—if that's all—there's nothing in that. (*She moves below the sofa and sits on it at the right end*) I thought you were dead. You don't think I should have married Claud if I'd known you were alive, do you?

DUDLEY (*moving to* L *of the sofa*) Of course not. And you had every justification for believing me dead. I appreciate that.

ANDREA. Well, then . . .

DUDLEY. But, unfortunately, dear, it's not what you believe that matters.

ANDREA. What does, then?

DUDLEY. The simple and undeniable fact that I'm alive.

ANDREA (*scornfully amused*) Well, really—you never were exactly logical, Dudley, but that's absurd. What on earth has that got to do with it? Of course you're alive—in fact. Nobody disputes that. But it's what you are in law that matters.

DUDLEY. What am I in law, then?

ANDREA. Dead as a door nail.

DUDLEY. Who says so?

ANDREA. Well, it stands to reason. You must be officially dead before anyone can be hanged for killing you.

DUDLEY (*mystified*) Who's been hanged?

ANDREA. As it happens, nobody. But I should have been, shouldn't I, if they had believed that girl. I mean, the law doesn't even try you for murder if it thinks the victim's still alive. That's common sense.

(DUDLEY *is now completely bemused*)

CLAUD (*moving down* C; *pessimistically*) Still, I doubt whether there's much in that argument, you know.

ANDREA (*to Claud; astonished*) Are you agreeing with him?

CLAUD. Not exactly, no, but . . .

ANDREA. What do you mean, then? Don't you want me, or what?

CLAUD. Of course I want you. It's no good shutting your eyes to facts, though.

ANDREA. Well, really, you talk as if you were perfectly ready to hand me over to the first Tom, Dick or Harry who comes along.

CLAUD (*harassed*) Not at all, I . . .

DUDLEY (*to Andrea; interrupting loudly*) *Look!* Would you mind telling me what the hell you're talking about? *What* murder?

ANDREA (*staring at Dudley*) Well, yours, of course.

DUDLEY (*after a thoughtful pause*) Well, I don't know. I suppose I'm being very stupid, but . . . (*He breaks off*)

ANDREA (*incredulously*) Do you mean that you don't know about it?

DUDLEY. Yes, I do mean that I don't know about it.

CLAUD (*moving above the sofa*) In that case, my friend, let me have the exquisite pleasure of telling you. While you were so callously engaged in keeping your continued existence a secret— your wife very nearly went to the gallows on your account.

DUDLEY (*thunderstruck*) What!

ANDREA (*to Claud; complainingly*) There you go again. I'm *not* his wife.

CLAUD (*irritably*) You were at that time, anyway. There can't be any doubt about that.

ANDREA. Yes, but . . .

DUDLEY (*to Andrea; interrupting*) Is this true?

ANDREA. Certainly it's true. (*She ticks off the events on her fingers*) I was confined to my stateroom by the captain, arrested when the ship got in, charged and committed before the Essex Justices at Tilbury, sent to Holloway to await trial, and tried at the Old Bailey.

(DUDLEY *is dumbfounded*)

CLAUD (*crossing down* R) And what's more—he knows it.

ANDREA. Now, why should you say that? He mightn't have seen the papers—especially in Africa. You didn't—even at Cheltenham.

DUDLEY (*unbelievingly*) They thought you'd killed me?

ANDREA. I've got the press cuttings, if you don't believe me.

(DUDLEY *sinks into the armchair down* L)

CLAUD. He would have made it his business to see the papers— wherever he was. Anyone would, who'd fallen off a ship.

DUDLEY (*rather weakly*) There weren't any papers where I was.

ANDREA (*to Claud*) See?

CLAUD. That's nonsense! There are papers everywhere nowadays.

ANDREA. Well, you're not suggesting he kept quiet on purpose, are you?

CLAUD (*sitting in the armchair down* R) I wouldn't put it past him.

ANDREA. But—why should he?

CLAUD. He may have wanted you to pay the extreme penalty, for all I know.

DUDLEY. Don't be so damn silly.

ANDREA (*to Claud; indignantly*) That would have been almost like murder.

DUDLEY (*defensively*) I didn't know a thing about it, Andrea.

ANDREA. I'm sure you didn't, dear. (*As if soliloquizing, and with less confidence*) It does seem a little odd, though, I must say.

DUDLEY. What's odd about it?

ANDREA. Well—it was even on the B.B.C.

CLAUD. Exactly! Where could he have been to get away from *that*?

DUDLEY (*rising and moving up* L; *sullenly*) All right! If you must know—I was—I was in prison.

ANDREA (*relieved*) There! I knew there must be some perfectly innocent explanation.

CLAUD. In prison where?

DUDLEY. Liberia.

CLAUD. How long for?

DUDLEY. Nine months. And if you want to know *what* for, you can mind your own business because that's got nothing to do with it.

ANDREA (*to Claud*) Now are you satisfied?

CLAUD (*grudgingly*) Certainly seems more likely than anything else he's said. I don't see why he shouldn't have written, though, to say he was alive, even if he didn't know what was going on.

DUDLEY (*righteously*) And disclose where I was? I've got some self-respect, you know.

CLAUD. That, I feel, is the most remarkable assertion yet.

(*Even the good-natured* DUDLEY *is getting tired of this hostility*)

DUDLEY (*crossing to* C) Look here—I thought you were supposed to be pleased to see me.

ANDREA (*to Dudley*) What on earth can have given you that idea?

DUDLEY. He said so.

(ANDREA *looks at Claud for an explanation*)

CLAUD (*uncomfortably*) Well, when he first came in, the only thing I could think of was that it showed that you—well, that you weren't a murderess.

ANDREA (*ominously*) Showed who?

CLAUD. Oh, not me, dear. The world in general.

ANDREA. Oh!

DUDLEY (*to Claud*) Actually, of course, it didn't show anything of the kind. All it did show was that she's not a successful murderess. (*He turns to the french windows*)

(CLAUD *is quite undismayed*)

ANDREA (*appealing to Claud*) There! Now, there's an example. You see how the man splits hairs. Can you wonder that I found him impossible to live with?

CLAUD (*after a reassuring gesture to Andrea; to Dudley*) You mean, she might have tried to kill you and failed?

DUDLEY (*maliciously*) For all *you* know. (*He sits on the left end of the window seat*)

ANDREA (*to Claud*) Take no notice, dear. He's only trying to get his own back.

CLAUD (*rising*) I know, I know. (*He moves to the downstage end of the window seat. To Dudley*) For all I know, she might have done, yes. But not for all you know, my friend. Indeed, you're the only person—apart from Andrea herself—who does know—for certain.

ANDREA. Well, if you have it in your mind to ask him, Claud, you'd better save your breath because, whatever the truth is, you'll only get one answer from him—and that is that I did.

DUDLEY (*resentfully perplexed*) What!

CLAUD (*a little startled*) Why?

ANDREA (*to Claud*) Because, obviously, dear, if he wants me back, he's going to give the answer best calculated to remove your competition.

CLAUD (*relaxing*) Oh!

ANDREA (*shaking a finger at Dudley*) I warn you, though, if you do say anything like that—after I've been found not guilty—I can have you for slander.

DUDLEY (*protestingly*) I haven't the slightest int——

CLAUD (*interrupting; with a satisfied air*) In any case, my dear, he's already answered the question by the very fact of wanting you back. No man—not even he—would want a wife he believed to be a killer—however rich she might be.

(ANDREA *does not seem particularly impressed.* DUDLEY *is not impressed at all; he looks like a man with a secret worry*)

ANDREA (*rising*) Well, if you're satisfied, dear, I'm sure I am. (*She crosses to Dudley*) And now, if you don't mind, both of you—I must go to bed.

(DUDLEY *rises*)

Good night, Dudley dear. (*She kisses him*) You are staying the night, I suppose?

(DUDLEY *seems a little taken by surprise*)

CLAUD (*incredulously*) Staying the night?

ANDREA (*to Claud*) He won't get in anywhere round here, dear.

(CLAUD *rolls his eyes to heaven and turns away down* R)

DUDLEY. Well, I have got a bag in the car, of course.

ANDREA. Then do. (*She crosses to the stairs*) You don't want to go all the way back tonight, and there is a room. Claud will show you. (*To Claud*) And then—don't be too long, will you, dear? It's been a heavy day.

(ANDREA *exits up the stairs.* DUDLEY *resumes his seat on the left end of the window seat.* CLAUD *crosses to the coffee table, picks up his glass, drains it, then moves to the sideboard and refills his glass*)

DUDLEY (*worried*) Look! What does she say, herself, about that?

CLAUD. About what?

DUDLEY. About whether she pushed me in. Doesn't she deny it?

CLAUD (*loftily*) Andrea would naturally regard it as beneath her dignity to answer such a question. What does it matter to you what she says, anyway? (*He looks at Dudley in sudden suspicion*) Don't you know whether she pushed you in?

(DUDLEY *looks uneasy and avoids Claud's eye*)

(*He picks up his drink and crosses to* L *of Dudley*) Don't you?

DUDLEY (*with a note of defiance*) No, as a matter of fact, I don't. (*He rises and moves down* R)

CLAUD (*following Dudley*) You don't?

DUDLEY. You see—there had been a bit of a party that night.

CLAUD (*horrified*) You mean you can't remember?

DUDLEY. Not a thing—until after I got in the sea. That seemed to sober me.

CLAUD. But think what you're saying, man. (*His dismay is monumental*)

DUDLEY. Well, I don't like it any more than you do.

CLAUD. It means that nobody knows—(*he indicates the staircase*) but *her.*

DUDLEY (*sitting in the armchair down* R; *gloomily*) I know.

CLAUD (*muttering*) Good heavens! (*He crosses thoughtfully down* L)

DUDLEY. What do you think yourself, though?

CLAUD. How the hell should I know? I only heard about it this evening. (*He sits in the armchair down* L)

DUDLEY. But, I mean, you know her. Is she the sort of woman you'd expect to do a thing like that?

CLAUD. I shouldn't have married her if she were, should I?

DUDLEY (*impressed*) That's true, you know.

CLAUD. You know her better than I do, anyway.

DUDLEY. What about it?

CLAUD. Well—what's your opinion?

DUDLEY (*brightening*) Well, if it comes to that, of course, I married her, too, didn't I?

CLAUD (*brightening*) That's right. You did.

DUDLEY (*rising and crossing down* C) Well, we can't both be wrong about her, can we?

CLAUD. Well, not as wrong as all that, surely.

DUDLEY. I mean, we're neither of us complete fools, are we?

CLAUD. No, we're men of experience.

DUDLEY. Judgement.

(*The atmosphere is getting quite gay*)

CLAUD. Of course. (*He drains his glass and rises*) Look! (*He takes Dudley's glass with his own to the sideboard*) Let's have another drink and talk it over sensibly.

DUDLEY (*sitting on the sofa at the left end*) By all means.

CLAUD (*refilling the glasses*) There's no need to get in a panic over a thing like this.

DUDLEY. None whatever. (*He ponders*) And there's another thing, you know.

CLAUD. Oh?

DUDLEY (*looking clever*) Now look. I don't know whether she pushed me, do I?

CLAUD (*picking up the glasses and moving below the sofa*) No.

DUDLEY (*craftily*) But she didn't know that, did she—until I told her?

CLAUD (*blankly*) Well? (*He hands a glass to Dudley*)

DUDLEY. Well, for all she knew, I was in a position to say she'd done it—if she had.

CLAUD (*sitting R of Dudley on the sofa*) What about it?

DUDLEY. She didn't seem concerned, that's all.

CLAUD. No, by Jove, she didn't, did she?

DUDLEY. Delighted to see me, in fact.

CLAUD (*very impressed*) I say, you know, you've got something pretty conclusive there.

DUDLEY (*looking smug*) *I* thought so.

CLAUD (*lifting his glass*) Well—your good health, Mr Nightshade.

DUDLEY (*lifting his glass*) And yours, Mr Merrilees.

(*They drink gaily*)

CLAUD (*soberly*) Look—I don't want to appear rude, but would you mind telling me—do you know the law when you say she's still your wife—or is that just your opinion?

DUDLEY. Well—I must admit—I don't know absolutely for certain. I did pop into a Public Reference Library for a few minutes this afternoon—but I didn't seem able to find the right book. Still, it seems common sense.

CLAUD. That, I must admit. (*With a flicker of hope*) However, the law is not always what one would expect.

DUDLEY. It isn't. For instance, you wouldn't expect to get nine months for trying to get into somebody's harem, would you?

CLAUD (*laughing*) Is that what you did?

DUDLEY (*laughing*) That's all.

CLAUD (*laughing*) Well, I'm blowed!

(*They enjoy the joke a moment longer, and take another drink*)

Well, obviously, the first thing to be done tomorrow is to see a lawyer and find out whose wife she is.

DUDLEY. Yes. (*He hesitates*) In the meantime . . . (*He breaks off*) CLAUD. Yes?

DUDLEY. It's going to be a bit awkward for you, isn't it?

CLAUD. In what way?

DUDLEY (*delicately*) Well, the er—the nuptials will have to be suspended *pro tem*, won't they?

CLAUD (*stiffening*) I naturally appreciate that.

DUDLEY. Yes, but—does she appreciate it, that's the point?

CLAUD (*coldly*) I think I have sufficient tact and delicacy to make it clear to her.

DUDLEY (*shrugging*) It's not the sort of thing *I* should care to have to make clear to Andrea. (*With a touch of malice*) *You* may find it easier, of course.

CLAUD (*rising and moving to the sideboard*) Well, as far as that goes—perhaps you'll be good enough to mind your own business. (*He puts down his glass*)

DUDLEY (*mildly*) But I think it's very much my business.

CLAUD (*moving to R of the sofa*) Only in so far as it concerns where you're going to spend the night.

DUDLEY (*mystified*) Where *I'm* going to spend the night?

CLAUD. Certainly. The first thing that becomes apparent is that I shall need the room *you* were going to have.

DUDLEY. Why?

CLAUD. Because it's the only other one in the house.

DUDLEY. Can't we share it?

CLAUD. It has only a single bed, my friend, and I don't propose to double up with you, I can assure you.

DUDLEY (*reasonably*) No, I do see that. That would be too much —after what you anticipated.—What do you suggest I do, then?

CLAUD. Ah—that's where it does become your business. (*He indicates the sofa*) You can have that if you like.

DUDLEY. This? (*He considers a moment*) No—I'm sorry—I shouldn't be comfortable.

CLAUD (*crossing to the staircase*) That's your business, too. It's all there is.

DUDLEY. I mean in my mind.

CLAUD (*stopping and turning*) What do you mean by that?

DUDLEY. You can't expect me to stop down here and leave a woman who's very likely my wife on the same landing as a man she persists in regarding as her husband. It isn't reasonable.

CLAUD (*moving above the sofa; furiously*) Are you suggesting that I should be such an unutterable cad as to take advantage of that?

DUDLEY (*calmly*) You might never even think of it, for all I know—but I should. (*He rises, wanders to the sideboard and refills his glass*) You see, I've got the sort of mind that does think of things like that. I shouldn't sleep a wink with you up there.

CLAUD (*crossing to L of Dudley*) In that case, you can take your car and spend your sleepless night somewhere else, because, if that's the sort of mind you've got, I won't even have you under the same roof as Andrea. I've at least been through a form of marriage with her, and, until you can prove anything to the contrary, I intend to regard her as my wife—even if I can't treat her as such. (*He crosses down L*)

DUDLEY (*incredulously*) And leave you here with her?

CLAUD. Certainly! I don't care a damn what you think. (*He sits in the armchair down L*)

DUDLEY (*picking up his glass and moving down C*) All right! Let's forget my feelings for the moment. We'll take it that I trust you, if you like. I'll come round tomorrow and believe you when you say you stopped in your room all night. How's that?

CLAUD. Very handsome of you.

DUDLEY. Nobody else will, though.

CLAUD. What do you mean?

DUDLEY. You only got married this morning, old man. You know what the world is.

CLAUD. Blast the world!

DUDLEY (*perching himself on the right arm of the sofa*) By all means. It was Andrea I was thinking of. I mean, if she *has* committed bigamy, at least let her be able to show that it's bigamy in name only. We don't want her having to change her name again, do we?

CLAUD. All right. I'll sit up in here all night.

DUDLEY (*pityingly*) My dear fellow—that's even more difficult to swallow.

CLAUD. Not if I've got a witness, it isn't.

DUDLEY. What witness?

CLAUD. You, my friend. If you're so jolly concerned about Andrea, you can damn well stop here and check up on me. You can still have the couch if you want it. I'll sit here.

DUDLEY. Oh no!

CLAUD. Why not?

DUDLEY. I'm a very heavy sleeper.

CLAUD (*jumping to his feet; angrily*) Now, look here . . .

DUDLEY (*interrupting*) Who's going to believe me, anyway, with my reputation?

(ANDREA *enters down the stairs. She is wearing a négligé*)

ANDREA (*as she enters*) Forgot the car after all.

CLAUD (*shouting at Dudley*) Then what the hell *do* you want me to do?

ANDREA (*crossing to* c) Dudley.

(DUDLEY *rises*)

You're not still on about being my husband, are you?
DUDLEY. Not exactly—no.
ANDREA. Then what are you wrangling about now? (*She looks from Dudley to Claud*)

(CLAUD *looks away*)

DUDLEY (*hesitating slightly*) It's something, my dear, which you —in your innocence—would not even have thought of.
ANDREA (*mystified*) Huh?

(DUDLEY, *moving with deliberation, goes to the sideboard, puts his glass on it, then moves to* R *of Andrea and takes her hands*)

DUDLEY (*acting*) Andrea—I don't blame you for marrying again—you know that, don't you? I even take it as a compliment —because it shows that there was at least something about married life that I taught you to appreciate.
ANDREA (*after a thoughtful pause*) I can't *think* of anything, dear.
CLAUD. What's all that got to do with it, anyway?
DUDLEY. I don't want her to think that what I'm going to point out to her is due to petty spite on my part, that's all.
CLAUD. I wasn't aware that anyone asked you to point out anything. And there's no need to hold her hands like that, either.
DUDLEY (*releasing Andrea's hands and moving down* R) All right. You tell her. But, if ever you're married to her as long as I was— you'll learn that it's sometimes wise to hold her hands.
ANDREA (*to Claud*) What *is* this?
CLAUD (*crossing to* L *of Andrea; acutely ill at ease*) Well, the fact is, Andrea—we both feel—he and I—that it would be better for all concerned if—just for the time being—until we've got things straightened out a bit . . .
ANDREA (*interrupting; warningly*) Claud—if it's anything at all to do with this idiotic claim of his . . .
DUDLEY (*intervening*) Darling—(*he crosses to* R *of Andrea*) it isn't. In fact, I want you to forget the whole thing. Look—pretend I haven't come yet. Put the clock back twenty-four hours and pre- tend it's yesterday, and then, as far as you're concerned, I'm still at the bottom of the sea. Now—how will that do?

(CLAUD *looks puzzled*)

ANDREA (*perplexed*) Well, it's terribly nice of you, Dudley, but —what's the point of it?
DUDLEY. I seem to have mucked things up a bit, that's all.

ANDREA. But if it is yesterday—that means that this morning's ceremony hasn't taken place yet.

DUDLEY. Well, naturally.

(CLAUD's *change of expression shows that he has cottoned on*)

ANDREA. Then, I'm still a widow.

DUDLEY. One must be consistent, of course.

ANDREA. But I shouldn't like that, dear.

DUDLEY. You can't have it both ways, Andrea.

CLAUD. You've been a widow for nearly a year. A day or so can't make much difference, surely.

ANDREA (*to Claud; with a suddenly hard eye*) Do *you* want to play this game?

CLAUD. I think it might help, dear, really. (*He takes Andrea's hands in emulation of Dudley*)

ANDREA. But, how can I pretend to be a widow when we're occupying the same room, Claud? It wouldn't be nice.

CLAUD. But, darling, that's just it. We both think—he and I, that—we shouldn't occupy the same room.

DUDLEY. Just for a day or so, that's all.

ANDREA (*ominously calm*) Does that mean—in plain language— that I'm to spend my wedding night alone?

CLAUD. Sounds awfully dreary, I know, but . . . (*He breaks off*)

ANDREA (*placidly*) Very well—since I'm outvoted—we'll *play* games and pretend I'm still a widow. (*She looks from one to the other*) But it's going to last longer than a *day* or so. (*With sudden ferocity*) I *promise* you—both.

(ANDREA, *on the word "promise" kicks* CLAUD *smartly on the shin, so that he releases her hands, enabling her to turn and, on the word "both", slap Dudley's face. She then crosses and exits angrily up the stairs.* CLAUD *hops to the right arm of the sofa and sits on it*)

DUDLEY (*holding his face*) See what I mean? (*He crosses to* R)

CLAUD (*thoughtfully rubbing his shin*) H'm! Rather surprising!

DUDLEY. Wouldn't think it, would you—to look at her? (*He sits on the left end of the window seat*)

CLAUD (*after a pause*) I say.

DUDLEY. Hm?

CLAUD. Do you know what botulism is?

DUDLEY (*faintly surprised*) Botulism? Sort of food poisoning. Why?

CLAUD. I just wondered.

DUDLEY. It's what her aunt died of.

CLAUD (*looking at Dudley*) I know.

DUDLEY (*rising; horrified*) Good heavens! You don't think . . . ?

a

A large suitcase hurtles down the staircase. Claud *jumps to his feet. A bowler hat and overcoat follow.* Claud *and* Dudley *look at each other. Then* Claud *goes solemnly up* L, *picks up the hat, puts it on, lifts the suitcase and looks at Dudley.* Dudley *crosses to the sofa and picks up his coat.*

Claud *and* Dudley *exit by the passage to the front door.*

As they exit a bag of golf-clubs descends the staircase with a crash, and a shooting-stick, camera-case, kitbag, tennis racquet, dressing-case, fishing-rod and a small suitcase follow in rapid succession as—

the Curtain *falls*

ACT II

SCENE—*The same. Tuesday evening, before dinner.*

When the CURTAIN *rises, it is daylight, but the sun is setting. The table* R *is almost fully laid with dinner things for three. The kitchen door is open and the usual music issues forth.* MRS O'CONNOR *is bending to burrow in the sideboard cupboard and her rear end is presented to the audience.*

MRS O'CONNOR (*shouting over the music*) It isn't a question of letting people live their own lives at all. (*She takes some table mats and cutlery from the cupboard and straightens up*) It's a question of whether they're fit to be at large. (*She crosses to the table* R) Of course, everyone has their own way of doing things. (*She lays out the mats and cutlery*) I know that as well as you do. But there is a point when the way you do things ceases to be normal, that's all— and hanging seaweed on the pictures is one of them—you can say what you like. (*She crosses to the sideboard*) So is throwing your things all over the floor and leaving them there all night. (*She takes a cruet from the sideboard cupboard*) And as for a man who goes back to London on his wedding night—well, *I* should have thought that *you*, of *all* people, would have considered that *most* abnormal. (*She crosses to the table* R) People do have their own way of doing things, but it's the first time I ever heard of anyone having that way of doing *that*. (*She puts the cruet on the table*)

(*The telephone bell rings*)

(*She crosses to the kitchen door*) That'll be her ladyship again, wanting to know if everybody's still appreciating how kind she is. (*She closes the kitchen door*)

(*The music ceases*)

(*She turns to the telephone and lifts the receiver. Into the telephone*) Hullo? . . . (*With a slightly offended air*) Yes, Mrs Fish . . . No, I'm sorry, she's out again, and Mr Merrilees is still in town. He did ring up this afternoon to ask if Mrs Merrilees could see him this evening—on business—and I don't know what he meant by that, I must say . . . But I've laid for him, and he hasn't come yet . . . Certainly I'll tell her, Mrs Fish . . . (*Sourly*) Oh, I'm sure she's most grateful. Good-bye. (*She replaces the receiver and opens the kitchen door*)

(*The radio music is heard*)

(She calls) There! Just as I said. She . . .

> *(There is a knock at the front door off)*

Oh, fiddle! *(She closes the kitchen door)*

> *(The music ceases.*
>   Mrs O'Connor *exits by the passage up* L. *The front door off is heard to open)*

Claud *(off)* Oh—good evening. Is Mrs Nightshade in?
Mrs O'Connor *(off)* Who?
Claud *(off)* Mrs Merrilees.
Mrs O'Connor *(off)* She's still on the beach.
Claud *(off)* Oh!
Mrs O'Connor *(off; after a slight pause)* Well, aren't you coming in?
Claud *(off)* Oh—thank you.

> *(*Claud *and* Dudley *enter by the passage up* L. Mrs O'Connor *follows them on. She has an angrily bewildered air. Both men now wear lounge suits.* Claud *carries a bowler hat, umbrella and brief-case. His manner is stiffly formal and he glances apprehensively up the staircase.* Dudley *wanders down* L)

(He crosses up RC. *To Mrs O'Connor)* Is she—er—is she expecting us?

Mrs O'Connor. I told her *you* were coming—if that's what you mean. *(She glances resentfully at Dudley)*
Claud. May we wait?
Mrs O'Connor. Well, of course you can wait if you want to. I thought you were living here. *(She rolls her eyes to heaven, moves to the kitchen door and turns)* And I hope you don't think it eccentric of me, Mr Merrilees, but I put all your—hockey-sticks and things upstairs again.

> *(*Mrs O'Connor *exits into the kitchen. Her exit is accompanied by the usual burst of music.* Claud *moves solemnly to the sofa, sits stiffly upright with hat, brief-case and umbrella on his lap. There is a short silence during which* Dudley *stares at Claud as if waiting)*

Dudley *(presently)* Well—have you made up your mind?

> *(*Claud *shifts unhappily and avoids Dudley's eye)*

(Kindly) Look, Claud—you heard what the man said. The first thing we've got to do is decide what we *want* to do. We can't move until we've done that. *I* want her—whatever she may or may not have done. There's something about Andrea that's not easy to give up. Now, I'm definite. What about you?
Claud. I don't know what to say. I—I love her—and yet there's this dreadful possibility which . . . *(He breaks off helplessly)*

DUDLEY. I know how you feel, of course, but . . . (*He breaks off*)

CLAUD (*tenderly reminiscent*) When I think of her warmth, her sweetness—when I think of the tenderness she displayed towards me on this very couch, only last night . . .

DUDLEY (*sympathetically*) You can't tell me, old man.

CLAUD. When I think of things like that, I—I just can't believe it of her—and yet . . . (*He breaks off*)

DUDLEY. I know. (*He moves up* L, *turns, and for a moment, regards Claud's back view with a grin, then, apparently on an impulse, moves to* R *of the sofa*) Claud—I'm going to give myself the luxury of doing something decent for a change.

CLAUD (*slightly startled*) Huh?

DUDLEY. You've been nice about all this. There was no need for you to take me with you to see counsel this afternoon—but you did—and I appreciate it. I'm going to tell you something. (*He pauses*) She didn't push me in. (*He looks away*)

CLAUD (*rising*) What?

DUDLEY (*apparently ashamed*) Did her best to save me, in fact.

CLAUD. But—but you said . . .

DUDLEY. I know I did. It wasn't true. (*He crosses to* R)

CLAUD. You *can* remember?

DUDLEY. Perfectly. I wasn't plastered—just lit-up.

CLAUD. I see. (*He sinks back on to the sofa*) You wanted me to doubt her. You wanted me out of your way.

DUDLEY. That's what it comes to.

CLAUD (*angrily*) Why didn't you make a job of it, then—and say she did push you in?

DUDLEY (*turning to him*) You wouldn't have believed it, old man.

CLAUD (*bitterly*) Why not? I seem to believe anything.

DUDLEY. It wouldn't have been credible, would it—seeing that I want her myself?

CLAUD (*grudgingly*) Oh, well, I'm glad you've told me, anyway. No doubt it's kindly meant. (*Gloomily*) I'm not sure it wouldn't have been kinder to let me go on doubting, though—with things as they are.

DUDLEY (*crossing to* R *of the sofa*) What do you mean—"with things as they are"? You mustn't be defeatist about it, Claud.

CLAUD. She's your wife and you want her. If that's not a handicap I don't know what is.

DUDLEY. But does she want me? That's what matters. So far it seems a bit doubtful.

CLAUD. All right. Supposing she doesn't want you. It doesn't follow that she's going to want me, does it?

DUDLEY. Not necessarily, no. But she's married you once. That's some encouragement, surely.

CLAUD. Suppose she does want me, then. Where do we go from there?

DUDLEY (*indicating the brief-case*) Look at your notes, old man, and see what Sir Henry said.

CLAUD (*putting his hat on the coffee table*) I know what Sir Henry said. (*He takes his spectacles from his pocket, and puts them on*) It's precisely that that I find so disheartening. (*He takes some papers from his brief-case and reads*) "In the event that it is the wish of the parties of the second marriage to remain together . . ."

DUDLEY (*leaning over Claud's shoulder*) That's you two.

CLAUD. Yes. ". . . and assuming that the legal husband is disposed to be generous . . ."

DUDLEY. That's me.

CLAUD (*a little testily*) Yes, all right. ". . . the only course open would appear to be—(a) dissolution of the first marriage . . ."

DUDLEY. That's mine.

CLAUD. ". . . and—(b) re-solemnization of the second."

DUDLEY. That's yours.

CLAUD (*replacing the notes in his brief-case*) Exactly.

DUDLEY (*straightening up*) In other words—a divorce for me—and your performance all over again. That's all. It's perfectly simple. (*He crosses down* R)

CLAUD (*replacing his spectacles in his pocket*) But, my good man, you can't get a divorce just like that. You've got to have grounds.

DUDLEY (*airily*) Oh, one can always rake up something.

CLAUD. That's all very well, but . . . (*He looks keenly at Dudley*) She hasn't any grounds, I suppose?

DUDLEY. Well, not just at the moment, perhaps—not that she knows of, anyway.

CLAUD. Well, you've nothing on *her*. I'm quite certain, so . . . (*He breaks off with a hopeless shrug*)

DUDLEY. I should have had, of course—if I hadn't turned up here when I did.

CLAUD. If what?

DUDLEY (*trying to be delicate*) Well, if I—if I hadn't mucked up your honeymoon.

CLAUD (*indignantly*) Are you implying that that would have given you grounds for divorcing her?

DUDLEY (*crossing to* R *of the sofa*) Well, look at your notes, old man.

(CLAUD *irritably takes the notes from the brief-case and as he puts on his spectacles,* DUDLEY *grabs the papers from Claud's lap*)

(*He looks at the notes*) There you are. (*He reads*) "Since the second marriage is invalid and therefore no marriage at all, its consummation would be adulterous and accordingly would provide grounds for the dissolution of the first . . ." (*He tosses the papers back to Claud*)

CLAUD (*replacing his spectacles in his pocket*) But—but that's preposterous.

DUDLEY. Seems to be the law, though. (*He wanders up* R)

CLAUD (*replacing the notes in the brief-case; fervently*) Thank God, then, that you arrived in time.

DUDLEY. Yes—if I did.

CLAUD (*looking sharply at Dudley*) What do you mean by that? You know you did, you were here soon after dinner.

DUDLEY (*gazing out of the french windows*) You'd had all the afternoon, though, hadn't you?

CLAUD (*rising with his umbrella and brief-case and crossing angrily to Dudley*) Now, look here, Nightshade—I don't know what you mean by that, but . . .

DUDLEY (*turning; interrupting*) Nobody would have blamed you, old man. You thought you were married.

CLAUD. I don't care what I thought. I'm not going to have you, or anyone else suggesting that I . . .

DUDLEY (*interrupting*) I'm not suggesting anything, anyway—except that you had the opportunity.

CLAUD. Why suggest even that? Don't you know when you're being offensive?

DUDLEY (*patiently*) Look! All I'm doing is to point out that, if she *does* want you, and I *am* disposed to be generous, there's my grounds for divorce, that's all—ready made. All you've got to do is say you stopped on the way down, or something. (*He moves down* R)

CLAUD (*incredulously*) Do you seriously believe that I would stand up in public and say a thing like that?

DUDLEY. I don't see why not. Nobody would be able to contradict you.

CLAUD (*moving to* L *of Dudley; outraged*) You don't see why not? On the way down? In daylight? Before dinner? You and I don't speak the same language, you know.

DUDLEY. Well, there's no need to get huffy about it, old man. I'm only trying to be decent.

CLAUD. Then I hesitate to think what your idea of indecency must be. (*He moves to the armchair down* R, *and sits stiffly, clinging to his brief-case and umbrella*)

(ANDREA *enters down the stairs. She wears a house-coat*)

ANDREA (*crossing to* C) Dudley!

DUDLEY (*moving to* R *of Andrea*) Hullo, darling.

(CLAUD *rises*)

ANDREA. How nice. I didn't expect *you*.

(DUDLEY *and* ANDREA *greet each other with a kiss*)

DUDLEY. We thought you were out.

ANDREA. No, I've been lying down, dear. I didn't sleep very well.

DUDLEY (*sympathetically*) I expect it's the silence.

ANDREA. Yes. Nobody breathing even. (*She glances coldly at Claud*) Good evening. (*She moves below the sofa*)

CLAUD. Good ev——

DUDLEY (*crossing to R of Andrea; interrupting*) Matter of fact, we were a little surprised to find you still here.

ANDREA (*surprised*) Surprised! But I came for a fortnight. (*She sits on the sofa*) Claud could have told you that.

CLAUD. Yes, but after—what's happened, I thought you'd very likely . . .

ANDREA (*interrupting; coldly*) I really don't know what justification you have for assuming that I'm going to change all my plans just because you don't appear to know your own mind.

(CLAUD *slowly re-seats himself in the armchair down* R)

(*To Dudley*) I shouldn't think of going off like that after Valerie Fish had been so kind as to lend us the house. She even had the bedroom done up specially.

DUDLEY. You're stopping on, then?

ANDREA. Somebody has to pretend to be enjoying themselves, Dudley.

DUDLEY (*perching himself on the right arm of the sofa*) But you'll be lonely.

ANDREA. Oh, not now, dear. I've sent for Aunt Gertrude.

DUDLEY (*delighted*) Gertrude! Oh, but that's a wonderful idea.

CLAUD. Who's Gertrude?

DUDLEY. Aunt Maggie's sister, dear boy. My favourite in-law.

CLAUD (*plaintively*) But I don't know who Maggie is.

ANDREA. You see, Claud, you don't even listen. Aunt Maggie's the one I told you about.

(CLAUD *looks blank*)

Died of botulism.

CLAUD. Oh! And this is her sister?

DUDLEY. Elder sister, believe it or not—and quite the most adorable thing you'll ever meet.

ANDREA. Yes. I'd forgotten what chums you used to be. Why don't you stay a few days and see something of her?

(CLAUD *stiffens*)

DUDLEY (*rising; warily*) Stay?

ANDREA. You might as well, dear.

DUDLEY. But—where am I going to sleep?

ANDREA. There's the guest-room.

DUDLEY. But if Gertrude's going to . . .

ANDREA (*interrupting*) Oh, she'll be in with me. That's what I got her for.

(CLAUD *and* DUDLEY *relax.* CLAUD *puts his umbrella and brief-case on the floor beside his chair*)

DUDLEY. Oh!

ANDREA (*innocently*) I can't bear sleeping alone. *You* know that.

DUDLEY. Yes. I remember. (*He grins*)

(ANDREA *looks at Dudley, then looks away in slight confusion and picks up an American magazine from the coffee table*)

(*He moves up* L) Well—I'll get my bag, then.

ANDREA. And while you're about it, Dudley . . .

DUDLEY (*stopping and turning*) Yes?

ANDREA. I think her train gets in about now.

DUDLEY. Right! I'll get her, too.

(ANDREA *relaxes into the right corner of the sofa and puts her feet up*)

ANDREA. Would you, dear? I wouldn't bother you, only Claud can't drive—either. (*She opens the magazine*)

DUDLEY. Of course. (*He hesitates and glances at Claud*) Before I go, though—(*to Claud*) would you mind stepping outside a moment, old man?

(CLAUD *solemnly collects his umbrella and brief-case, rises and goes out on to the sun-deck*)

(*He moves to* R *of the sofa*) Aren't you being a bit rough on the man?

ANDREA. After his behaviour last night, I think it's extremely nice of me to recognize his existence at all.

DUDLEY. Well, I know how you must feel, but . . .

ANDREA (*interrupting*) No woman with any self-respect could possibly overlook such conduct.

DUDLEY. I know, but . . .

ANDREA (*interrupting*) Refusing to spend the night with me like that.

DUDLEY. There was nothing else he could do.

ANDREA. Well, of course there wasn't. I know that. He acted with the utmost discretion. But you can't expect me to like it, Dudley. It's so rude.

DUDLEY. Well—try to be charitable, dear. He hasn't really done anything, remember.

ANDREA (*muttering*) No—that's just it.

DUDLEY (*turning and calling*) All right, old man. (*He moves up* L)

ANDREA. Come to think of it, though . . . (*She breaks off*)

DUDLEY (*stopping and turning*) Yes?

ANDREA. Why are *you* defending Claud?

DUDLEY (*in a slightly hurt tone*) Even I have some sense of justice, Andrea.

ANDREA. Oh yes, dear, I'm not being critical. It shows a nice spirit. I just can't see what you're up to, that's all.

(CLAUD *comes in from the sun-deck*)

DUDLEY (*abandoning his wounded air and grinning*) You will.

(DUDLEY *exits by the passage up* L. CLAUD *moves down* RC *and stands unhappily hesitant.* ANDREA *becomes absorbed in the magazine*)

CLAUD (*after a pause*) You're still cross with me, then?
ANDREA (*absently*) Um?
CLAUD. I say you're still . . .
ANDREA (*interrupting*) I do love these American advertisements for "intestinal regulators" and that sort of thing, don't you? They're so uninhibited. (*She looks up*) What did you say?
CLAUD. I said you're still cross with me.
ANDREA (*surprised*) Am I? What makes you think that?
CLAUD. I can tell by the way you treat me, Andrea.
ANDREA. You're getting too sensitive, Claud. (*She returns to the magazine*)
CLAUD. Well, may I proceed?
ANDREA (*looking up; faintly surprised*) Oh, was there something else you wanted to say?
CLAUD. I have to explain the legal position, Andrea.
ANDREA. Oh! (*She returns to the magazine*)
CLAUD. That's why I'm here.
ANDREA. I had wondered, I must say. (*In a bored tone*) Well? (*She begins searching for her handkerchief*)

(CLAUD *crosses to the armchair down* R, *sits, puts the umbrella on the floor and opens the brief-case*)

CLAUD. Well—we've seen a lawyer, and . . .

(CLAUD *becomes aware of* ANDREA'S *preoccupation. Having searched her person, she is now looking under the cushions and between the upholstery of the sofa.* CLAUD *watches with growing exasperation. Finally she finds the handkerchief behind a cushion, elaborately unfolds it and dabs delicately at her nose*)

As I was saying—we've seen a . . .

(ANDREA *loudly blows her nose*)

(*He waits until Andrea has finished mopping. Sarcastically*) Would you prefer me to come back another time?
ANDREA (*startled*) What? Good heavens, no! What a very disquieting idea. (*She again takes up the magazine*)
CLAUD (*rising; angrily*) Then, *please* listen.

A REA (*innocently*) I *am* listening. I've heard every word you've said. You've seen a lawyer.

CLAUD. Yes, I know, but . . .

ANDREA (*interrupting*) Get on with it, then. (*She returns to the magazine*)

CLAUD. A very eminent lawyer. Sir Henry Sutton-White, as a matter of fact.

ANDREA (*muttering*) Never heard of him.

CLAUD. Well, whether you've heard of him or not, Andrea, he's an authority whose dictum is not to be taken lightly, and you'd better pay some heed to what he says. (*He resumes his seat*)

(ANDREA *begins idly clicking her tongue*)

He specializes in this sort of thing. (*He pauses and stares angrily at her*)

(ANDREA *continues the clicking for a moment then glances up*)

ANDREA. All right! All right! I'm "heeding". What does he say?

CLAUD. Well, the first thing that becomes apparent is that it's a very unusual case.

ANDREA. I shouldn't have thought you needed an expert to tell you that.

CLAUD. The point is, Andrea, that it's so unusual as to be without precedent.

ANDREA. You mean it hasn't happened before?

CLAUD. Apparently not.

ANDREA (*gratified*) Well! Imagine that.

CLAUD. Not quite like this, anyway.

ANDREA. Women thinking that their husbands were dead for no better reason than that they'd been tried for killing them, you mean?

CLAUD. Er—yes.

ANDREA (*returning to the magazine*) Well, *I* don't see how he makes a living.

CLAUD. Who?

ANDREA. Sir Henry Thingummy-Whatsisname. I mean, if he specializes in the sort of thing that never happens, how can he hope to?—Doesn't sound very bright to me.

CLAUD (*putting his brief-case on the floor and rising*) I think you're being flippant, Andrea—and I think you're doing it deliberately in order to show that you no longer like me very much. (*He crosses to* C)

ANDREA. For a man, you know, Claud, you do have the most blinding flashes of intuition.

CLAUD. Is it worth my while to go on?

ANDREA. You've nothing to lose, I suppose.

CLAUD (*crossing to* L) With your permission, then, I'll be as brief as I can. I won't deny that, on certain points, Sir Henry was reluctant to commit himself then and there, and I suspect that even he needed time to refer to his books—but of one thing, Andrea, there is no possible shadow of doubt whatever.

ANDREA (*without interest*) Oh?

CLAUD (*moving to L of the sofa*) You're married to Dudley.

ANDREA (*looking up in weary surprise*) My dear Claud, you didn't come all the way down here to tell me that, did you?

CLAUD (*incredulously*) You mean you've accepted that?

ANDREA. It's indisputable.

CLAUD. But, last night, nothing would convince you that you were still his wife.

ANDREA. Well, I've slept on it.

CLAUD. I dare say, but . . .

ANDREA. *And* taken advice, if you want to know.

CLAUD. Oh, you have.

ANDREA. I haven't been entirely inactive myself, Claud. After all, I am an interested party.—I've been on to Valerie Fish.

CLAUD (*puzzled*) Valerie Fish?

ANDREA. Yes.

CLAUD. Is she a lawyer?

ANDREA. She is not.

CLAUD (*crossing to R; sarcastically*) Oh, just happens to know about these things, I suppose.

ANDREA. Well, she should do. She was married to a lawyer.— She didn't have to look it up, anyway, like your man. *She* knew at once.

CLAUD (*taking a grip on himself*) Well, anyway, she concurred.

ANDREA. Absolutely.

CLAUD. And you accept the fact that you're married to Dudley?

ANDREA. Technically—yes.

CLAUD (*sitting in the armchair down R*) The particular attitude you elect to adopt towards your husband is, of course, none of my business. (*He picks up his brief-case and puts on his spectacles*) All that concerns me is what you intend to *do* about me—and that, I think, you make abundantly clear.

(ANDREA *makes no comment, but she no longer looks at the magazine*)

(*He takes the notes from the brief-case*) If you *had* wanted to—er— to continue with me, there would have been very considerable complications—but, as it is, they do not arise, and—(*he looks at the notes*) all that you will need to do will be—"(a) . . ."

ANDREA. I didn't speak.

CLAUD. The letter A.

ANDREA. Eh?

CLAUD (*loudly*) A.

ANDREA. Oh!

CLAUD (*reading*) ". . . to apply to the court for the second marriage to be declared null and void *ab initio*."

ANDREA. Bless you!

CLAUD (*replacing the papers in the brief-case and removing his spectacles*) This is nothing more than a formality, and apparently not even necessary—merely wise. (*He picks up his umbrella and rises*) Which means, no doubt, that you won't trouble to do it at all. (*He crosses to* R *of the coffee table*)

ANDREA (*a little sulkily*) What's B then?

CLAUD. Forget that I ever existed. (*He picks up his hat from the coffee table, puts on his hat and holds out his hand*) Good-bye.

ANDREA. Well, I must say . . .

CLAUD. What? (*He withdraws his hand and removes his hat*)

ANDREA. You *are* an extraordinary man. (*She rises*) Who said anything about not wanting to go on with you? (*She puts the magazine on the coffee table*)

CLAUD. Well, nobody, but . . .

ANDREA. Then why on earth assume that I don't?

CLAUD. Well, you certainly haven't said that you do, Andrea.

ANDREA. But, I haven't been asked. You can't expect me to answer a question if you don't even put it to me, Claud.

CLAUD. Does that mean that you do want to go on with me?

ANDREA (*moving down* L) No, I'm not sure that it does—now.

CLAUD (*crossing to* R *of her*) But, Andrea . . .

ANDREA. Anyone might think you were trying to get out of it, the way you go on.

CLAUD. But, listen . . .

ANDREA (*turning; accusingly*) I expect that's what you are doing, come to think of it. You can't satisfy yourself that I didn't try to kill Dudley—that's what it is—and you're making use of a mere technicality to get rid of me. It's contemptible! (*She turns her back to him*)

CLAUD (*shouting*) But it isn't that. I don't want to get rid of you.

ANDREA. Simply because of a . . . (*She breaks off and turns to him in surprise*) You don't?

CLAUD. As it happens, I *am* satisfied that you didn't try to kill Dudley.

ANDREA. You are?

CLAUD. I don't think it would make any difference if you had killed him, anyway. It's the sort of thing anyone might do.

ANDREA. You mean that? (*She takes his arm*)

CLAUD (*cooling down, but still severe*) In any case, I don't care what you may or may not have done. I—I love you, Andrea. I've told you that before.

ANDREA (*nestling to him*) Oh, I'm so glad to hear it again though, Claud.

(CLAUD, *with his hat in one hand, and the umbrella and brief-case in the other, puts his arms around Andrea, but continues to grumble*)

CLAUD. It's ridiculous to say I don't want you. Of course I want you. But you're another man's wife. One must be objective about it. I oughtn't even to be standing here like this.

ANDREA (*enraptured*) Oh, you are sweet, really. I do see why I married you. (*She kisses him*) Come!

(ANDREA *draws* CLAUD *to the armchair down* L, *thrusts him into it, takes the umbrella and brief-case from him, puts them on the floor below the chair, then seats herself on his lap with an arm about his neck*)

CLAUD. Excuse me. (*He passes his hat across her from his right hand to his left and puts the hat with the brief-case*)

ANDREA. Will it mean an awful lot of bother? (*She kisses him on the forehead*)

CLAUD. What?

ANDREA. If we—decide to go on.

CLAUD (*still faintly hurt*) Not if you want me, of course.

ANDREA. Just a matter of getting rid of him, I suppose.

CLAUD. And re-marrying me.

ANDREA. Oh, shall we have to do that?

CLAUD. Naturally.

ANDREA (*delighted*) Another wedding? Oh, what fun! Where shall we have it this time?

CLAUD. It doesn't make any . . .

ANDREA (*interrupting*) And where shall we go for our honeymoon? Here again? Or would you like to try somewhere else for a change?

CLAUD. I don't . . .

ANDREA (*interrupting*) Well, we'll have the reception somewhere else, anyway. The *vol-au-vent* was awful, I thought, and even the . . . (*Suddenly thoughtful*) Claud.

CLAUD. Yes?

ANDREA. Shall we have to ask *him*?

CLAUD. I can't see that it matters. Why?

ANDREA. I don't want to cultivate him, dear. He's always a source of anxiety. Now, for instance . . . (*She breaks off, looking disturbed*)

CLAUD (*faintly alarmed*) What?

ANDREA. Have you noticed how nice he's being to you?

CLAUD. Matter of fact, I have rather, but—what about it?

ANDREA. Well, it's so surprising. I can't think why.

CLAUD (*still a little touchy*) I don't see that it's necessarily surprising.

ANDREA. Oh, no, dear, of course not. I'm sure he's very fond of you. I can't think that it's entirely on account of that, that's all. —Does he know you're well off?

CLAUD. What's that got to do with it?

ANDREA. Well, it nearly always is a matter of money when he does something you can't account for.

CLAUD (*complacently*) He won't get any out of me, I can assure you.

ANDREA. Well, do be careful, dear, won't you? He's awfully good at it, and I shouldn't like you to be done. After all, I do feel a little responsible for you. You did meet him through me, didn't you? (*She kisses him on the temple and lays her face against his*)

(GERTRUDE *and* DUDLEY *enter by the passage up* L. GERTRUDE PIGEON *is small, old, gentle, innocent and brisk. A blood-relation of Andrea, she has much in common mentally. In appearance she is countrified. She wears a light overcoat, a flowered cotton dress and a floppy straw hat. She is quite deaf except when using her home-made hearing aid. Always with her is a large and apparently weighty black plastic carrier bag. Clamped to her head is an ordinary one-sided ear-phone. This is connected by heavy flex to the apparatus within the bag, and at a convenient point on the flex is a massive switch which emits a very audible "clack" whenever used. She also carries a cricket bat.* DUDLEY *carries two suitcases and Claud's raincoat.* GERTRUDE *and* DUDLEY *pause for a moment to admire the group on the armchair down* L)

GERTRUDE (*crossing up* C) Andrea!

ANDREA (*scrambling to her feet and running to Gertrude*) Darling!

(CLAUD *rises hurriedly and in some confusion.* DUDLEY *grins at Claud and puts the cases and raincoat on the floor up* L)

(*She embraces Gertrude*) Oh, it is lovely to see you. (*She kisses her*)

GERTRUDE. Just a minute. (*She puts the cricket bat along the back of the sofa, clacks the switch and holds the bag towards Andrea*) What did you say?

ANDREA (*talking into the bag loudly*) It's lovely to see you.

GERTRUDE. Yes, dear, but there's no need to shout. (*She indicates the apparatus*) It's very powerful.

ANDREA. Oh!

GERTRUDE (*turning and smiling fondly at Dudley*) What a surprise you have for me.

(DUDLEY *moves to* L *of Gertrude and puts an arm about her shoulders*)

ANDREA. Yes, isn't it?

GERTRUDE. I could hardly credit my senses.

ANDREA. I know.

GERTRUDE (*beaming*) My first thought was that I must be dead, too.

DUDLEY (*laughing*) I'm afraid you and I would never meet in the same place, darling.

GERTRUDE (*to Andrea*) I felt so sure he was dead.

ANDREA (*laughing*) It just confirms what you've always said about him, Aunt Gertrude, you can't rely on a thing he does.

GERTRUDE (*with no trace of reproof*) No, but don't say anything unnecessary, dear. It wastes the batteries. (*She indicates Claud*) Who's this, then, that you were sitting with?

ANDREA. Oh, I'm so sorry. It's Claud. (*To Claud*) This is Aunt Gertrude, dear. Miss Pigeon. (*To Gertrude. Proudly*) He used to play for Kent.

(CLAUD and GERTRUDE *advance to meet each other below the sofa.* DUDLEY, *grinning, moves down* L)

CLAUD (*holding out his hand*) How do you do?

GERTRUDE (*taking his hand and holding it*) Oh, you're the new husband, I suppose?

CLAUD. Well—er . . .

ANDREA (*interposing*) In a way, dear, yes.

GERTRUDE (*smiling at Claud*) I'm glad to meet you. I hope you're strong. (*She releases his hand*)

(CLAUD *gives Dudley an anxiously puzzled look.* DUDLEY *shrugs lightly*)

(*To Andrea*) He's nice, isn't he? (*She sits on the sofa*) What did you say his name was?

ANDREA. Claud.

GERTRUDE. Claud what, though? I must learn it, I may have to write to you some time.

ANDREA. Merrilees.

GERTRUDE. Oh yes—Merrilees. (*She switches off, closes her eyes, puts her fingers to her brow and begins to repeat the name to herself*)

CLAUD (*to Gertrude; anxiously*) But you do realize, I suppose, that . . . ?

(GERTRUDE, *having switched off, does not hear what is said*)

DUDLEY (*interrupting*) I wouldn't bother, old man. Not just now.

CLAUD. But we can't let her go on thinking that I . . .

DUDLEY (*interrupting*) She's switched off, anyway.

GERTRUDE (*muttering*) Merrilees, Merrilees.

(ANDREA *moves to* R *of the sofa and pokes Gertrude.* CLAUD *moves down* L *and stands below Dudley*)

(*She opens her eyes and switches on*) Yes, dear?

ANDREA. It's the same name as the man who used to wind your clocks.

GERTRUDE. Oh, yes. So it is. How lucky! I can remember it by that. Is there anything else you wanted to say?

ANDREA. I don't think so. Not at the moment.

GERTRUDE. Then I'll write a letter. (*She switches off, takes a writing-pad and fountain pen from her bag, and begins to write*)

ANDREA (*to Dudley*) Well, perhaps you wouldn't mind taking her bag up, dear.

DUDLEY. Right. (*He moves up* L *and picks up a suitcase*) Which is her room?

ANDREA. Oh, of course—you haven't been upstairs yet, have you?

DUDLEY. No.

CLAUD (*moving up* L) I'll do it.

ANDREA (*to Claud*) Then show him his own room, too, dear, will you?

CLAUD (*picking up the second suitcase and the coat*) Here—this is my suitcase that you've brought in. My coat, too.

DUDLEY (*looking a little self-conscious*) Yes, I—well, to tell you the truth, I felt a bit mean about stopping here and letting you push off alone. I just felt that if anyone was going to spend the night, it ought to be you—particularly as the house was—put at your disposal in the first place. (*To Andrea. Meaningly*) I take it *you* don't mind?

ANDREA (*puzzled*) Well, no, I . . . (*She breaks off and stares suspiciously at Dudley*)

DUDLEY. Right! Then I needn't trouble to go up at all, need I? (*He hands the suitcase to Claud*)

CLAUD (*surprised*) I thought you objected to the idea of my spending the night.

DUDLEY. Not with Aunt Gertrude here, old man. I'm not all that prim.

CLAUD. Well, then—thanks.

(CLAUD *exits up the stairs, taking the suitcases and coat with him.* DUDLEY *moves and sits on the left arm of the sofa.* ANDREA *perches on the right arm of the sofa*)

DUDLEY (*touching the flex*) What is this contraption she's got on?

GERTRUDE (*looking up and switching on*) What, dear?

DUDLEY. Got a new aid, I see.

GERTRUDE. Henry made it for me.

ANDREA. Who's Henry?

GERTRUDE. A boy, dear. Fifteen. Belongs to the man who does the hedges. Such a pet, and so clever with his hands. Did this out of an old wireless, that's all. That, and a pressure-cooker, I think he said. Isn't it lovely? (*She holds up the bag*) Its works are all in here.

ANDREA (*peering into the bag*) Well, isn't that convenient?

GERTRUDE. You wouldn't believe how much better it is than that silly little thing I gave forty-five guineas for.

ANDREA. What do you mean by better, dear—louder?

D

GERTRUDE. Oh, *much* louder. It's *deaf*ening. (*She smiles, switches off, and goes on writing*)

(CLAUD *enters down the stairs and remains uncertainly at the foot.* ANDREA *rises, moves above the sofa and pokes Gertrude*)

(*She switches on*) Yes?

ANDREA. Wouldn't you like to see your room?

GERTRUDE (*replacing the pad and pen in the bag; enthusiastically*) Oh, yes, Andrea. What a lovely idea.

DUDLEY (*picking up the cricket bat*) What's this?

GERTRUDE. Oh, that's for Henry. He wanted a cricket bat. (*Anxiously*) It *is* a cricket bat, isn't it?

DUDLEY. Certainly it's a cricket bat.

GERTRUDE. Oh, I'm so glad. (*She rises and sets off down* R) I got it on my way through town.

(DUDLEY *rises and moves* L)

ANDREA (*indicating the staircase*) Up here, dear.

GERTRUDE. Oh! (*She changes direction, goes up* L, *then suddenly stops and turns. To Andrea*) Oh, you sent for me, didn't you? What did you want me for?

ANDREA. Only to sleep with me, Aunt Gertrude.

GERTRUDE (*puzzled*) Sleep with you? (*She looks at Claud*)

ANDREA. You know how nervous I am in a strange bed.

GERTRUDE (*after a thoughtful pause*) Well, you know—that's *most* odd.

ANDREA. What is, dear?

GERTRUDE (*shrugging*) Well—either things have changed considerably or my memory's playing me tricks, that's all.

(GERTRUDE *exits up the stairs.* ANDREA *crosses to the staircase*)

DUDLEY (*handing the cricket bat to Andrea*) Here!

(ANDREA *exits up the stairs.* DUDLEY *crosses to the sideboard*)

Drink?

CLAUD. No, thanks. (*He wanders down* R)

DUDLEY (*pouring a whisky and soda for himself*) Do you think Mrs Fish would mind if I had one?

CLAUD (*adjusting his tie in the mirror down* R) I shouldn't think so—especially as it happens to be mine.

DUDLEY. Oh, I'm so sorry, my dear fellow, I . . .

CLAUD (*interrupting*) Drink it! Drink it! Who cares? (*He sits moodily in the armchair down* R)

(DUDLEY *looks at Claud and grins craftily to himself. Then adjusting his face to an appropriate gravity, he moves and perches himself on the right arm of the sofa*)

DUDLEY. Well—you've had a chat, I take it?

CLAUD (*without looking at Dudley*) We have.

DUDLEY. You—learnt her wishes?

CLAUD. I did.

DUDLEY. And . . . ?

CLAUD. She wants me.

DUDLEY (*apparently stricken*) I see. (*He rises, moves up c and stands with his back to Claud*)

CLAUD (*after a pause; sincerely*) I'm sorry, Nightshade. I'm terribly sorry.

DUDLEY. It's all in the luck of the game. (*He sighs*) Ah, well. (*He drains his glass, puts it on the sideboard and turns, putting on a brave front*) Then why the worried look? (*He crosses to L of the sofa*)

CLAUD (*with distaste*) I don't like having to "rake up something", as you call it, for this divorce. It's unsavoury. I don't like being associated with it, even.

DUDLEY. It's only a matter of a receipted bill from the *Hotel Mizpah*, Bloomsbury—or something like that.

CLAUD. I know, but . . . (*He breaks off*)

DUDLEY. You want me to do it—is that what you mean?

CLAUD. Do what?

DUDLEY. Get the receipt, old man.

CLAUD (*astounded*) Well, good heavens, you wouldn't expect her to, would you?

DUDLEY. You don't see yourself as a co-respondent, I take it?

CLAUD (*rising and crossing to c*) I do not see myself as a co-respondent. But that has nothing to do with it. The woman is never expected to provide the evidence. It's a matter of chivalry.

DUDLEY (*crossing to L of Claud; patiently*) Look—the sooner you get it out of your head that you're dealing with anything remotely resembling a gentleman, the better—because you're not, you know.

CLAUD (*moving up c*) I'm sorry. I keep on forgetting.

DUDLEY (*crossing down R; kindly*) Well, do try to hold it in mind, old man, or we shan't get anywhere. (*He sits in the armchair down R*) Now—where were we?

CLAUD (*sullenly*) Hotel bill.

DUDLEY. Right! So with that from me and a few extra details from the chambermaid—Andrea gets her . . . (*He breaks off, suddenly looking doubtful*) No, that can't be right.

CLAUD. What can't be right?

DUDLEY. Well, Andrea gets her freedom . . .

CLAUD. Yes.

DUDLEY. You get Andrea . . .

CLAUD. Yes.

DUDLEY. But, what do I get?

CLAUD (*moving down c; puzzled*) What do *you* get?

DUDLEY. Yes—apart from a rather sordid evening's entertainment at the *Hotel Mizpah*—what do I get in return?

CLAUD. In return for what?

DUDLEY (*in apparent surprise*) My wife, old man.

CLAUD. What *can* you get in return for your wife?

(DUDLEY *considers for a moment, as if the question had not previously occurred to him*)

DUDLEY. You know—it's a pitiful thought, but there *is* nothing, is there, except money?

CLAUD. Ah—now I begin to see. (*Bitterly sarcastic*) I'm sorry. I hadn't realized you were putting her up for sale. And the price?

DUDLEY. Haven't really thought about it. Ten thousand?

CLAUD. Sounds to me as if you've thought about it quite a lot. That's C.O.D., I take it?

DUDLEY. Certainly, old man! I'd trust you anywhere.

CLAUD. Thanks! And what about payment? Cash—or would you take a cheque?

DUDLEY (*shrugging*) I'm not fussy.

CLAUD. No—I don't think you can be. (*He crosses deliberately to Dudley*) May I say, I think you are the most unmitigated blackguard I ever met? (*He turns, moves to the left end of the window seat and sits*)

DUDLEY (*mildly*) Well—now you can see the point of keeping that in mind. With me, you can discuss a thing like this—without embarrassment—without restraint. But how would you feel in the case of, say, Sir Henry Sutton-White, if you wanted to buy his wife?

(MRS O'CONNOR *enters from the kitchen. She carries a tray with a glass and side plate. For once, the radio off is silent. She crosses towards the table* R)

CLAUD (*unaware of Mrs O'Connor; violently*) Well, I don't want to buy Sir Henry's wife.

(MRS O'CONNOR *stops abruptly and stares at Claud.* DUDLEY *tries to signal her presence*)

I don't want to buy anyone's wife, and you can put that in your ... (*He sees Dudley's signals, turns, sees Mrs O'Connor, and abruptly shouts with nervous laughter*)

(MRS O'CONNOR, *scared, turns and exits hurriedly into the kitchen*)

(*He rises quickly. Furiously*) Now, you listen to me, Nightshade ...

GERTRUDE (*off upstairs*) Oh no, dear, I'm never without it.

(GERTRUDE *and* ANDREA *enter down the stairs.* GERTRUDE *has removed her hat and overcoat.* ANDREA *moves above the sofa.* GERTRUDE *moves below the sofa*)

DUDLEY (*rising*) Talk to you later, old man. (*He goes on to the sun-deck and sits in one of the chairs*)

ANDREA. Where does it come from, then—the chemist or the ironmonger, or what?

(CLAUD *moves to the armchair down* R *and sits*)

GERTRUDE (*sitting on the sofa at the right end*) No, it comes from a Peruvian weed, dear—Pettacattel. The natives make it. It's nothing to look at, of course, like so many things that are helpful. (*She rummages in her bag*) I'll show you. Just a brown powder, that's all. (*She takes a small, folded white paper from her bag*) There! Though that's only the paper it's done up in, of course. (*She replaces the paper in the bag*)

ANDREA. But what do you do with it, dear?

GERTRUDE. Well, personally, I drink it with my milk, but . . .

ANDREA. What's it for, though?

GERTRUDE. Oh, I see what you mean. Well, the natives use it as a sort of gum for sticking their hair, but I take it for headaches and rheumatism. Do you know what a llama is?

ANDREA. Sort of South American camel.

GERTRUDE. That's it. But what I dare say you don't know is that—(*weightily*) this weed Pettacattel is the llama's favourite food.

ANDREA. Is it?

GERTRUDE. It is. And it was your own great-uncle Lambert, dear—that most sagacious of men—though never really understood in his day—who first saw the significance of that. (*She takes her writing-pad and pen from the bag*)

ANDREA (*bewildered*) What *is* the significance of it?

GERTRUDE. Have you ever heard of a llama suffering from headaches or rheumatism?

ANDREA. No, I can't say I have.

GERTRUDE (*in mild triumph*) Well! (*She switches off and begins to write*)

ANDREA (*to Claud; puzzled*) Well—can *you* see the . . . ? (*She takes in Claud's moody appearance, glances towards the sun-deck, then crosses to* L *of Claud*) Have you found out what he was up to, Claud? Because that's what you look like.

CLAUD (*grimly*) I have.

ANDREA. *Was* it money?

CLAUD. It was.

ANDREA. Just a minute. (*She crosses to Gertrude, stoops and speaks loudly into her ear*) You *are* switched off, dear, aren't you? (*She pauses*)

(GERTRUDE *goes on placidly writing*)

(*She crosses to Claud*) All right! Go on.

CLAUD. He wants me to purchase you, Andrea.

ANDREA (*uncomprehendingly*) Purchase me!

CLAUD. He wants me to pay him a sum of money in return for the right to marry you.

ANDREA. Oh, for my freedom, you mean?

CLAUD. That is what I mean.

ANDREA (*ominously*) So, that's what it is. That's why he's "being fair", and taking your part, and throwing the two of us together. I see. (*She moves to the french windows and calls*) Dudley.

(DUDLEY *rises*)

(*She returns to Claud*) Oh, darling, I am sorry. I do feel so ashamed of him sometimes.

DUDLEY (*standing in the open windows*) Yes, dear?

ANDREA (*sweetly*) Would you come here a minute?

(DUDLEY *moves to* L *of Andrea*)

DUDLEY (*apprehensively*) Yes, dear?

ANDREA (*with restraint*) Dudley—I don't mind when you come back from the dead. (*She advances slowly on Dudley*)

(DUDLEY *backs away from Andrea and casts an anxious glance in the direction of Gertrude*)

You can't help being alive; I realize that—and it's not your fault that you still happen to be my husband. (*Suddenly and furiously*) But when you start using the situation——

(DUDLEY *crosses hurriedly above the sofa, passes round the left end of it, and sits* L *of Gertrude. He puts an arm about her, as if seeking protection.* GERTRUDE *looks at him, smiles vaguely, pats his hand, then goes on writing*)

(*she stands* R *of the sofa*) —to take advantage of a man like Claud, simply because you think he's rich and easily put upon—(*she leans over and shouts across Gertrude*) *that* I will not have. D'you understand?

DUDLEY (*cringing behind Gertrude*) Yes, dear.

ANDREA. Very well, then. (*She pauses. To Claud*) How much is he asking, anyway?

CLAUD (*irritably*) What does that matter? It doesn't make any difference what he's asking.

ANDREA (*crossing to Claud; firmly*) Darling, you may be ready to pay almost anything for me, but . . .

CLAUD (*interrupting; uncomfortably*) I don't mean that, Andrea.

ANDREA. What do you mean, then, dear?

CLAUD. I'm not going to pay him at all.

ANDREA (*crossing to* C; *with less enthusiasm*) Oh! Well, that's all right, then—so long as you *can* take care of yourself. But don't you hesitate to tell me if he does start again, Claud. (*She looks severely at Dudley*) I never heard of such a thing. (*She pauses. Trying not to sound curious*) Er—how much did he want for me, though?

DUDLEY (*rising*) Well, I did think about ten thousand. (*He moves down* L)

ANDREA (*secretly gratified, but trying to sound horrified*) Ten thousand!

DUDLEY. Yes.

ANDREA. Pounds?

DUDLEY. Certainly.

ANDREA (*with diminished conviction*) It's outrageous. Don't you pay it, Claud.

CLAUD. I'm not going to, Andrea. I've just been saying so.

(ANDREA *begins to look a little straight down her nose*)

DUDLEY. But, now that I look at you, Andrea—I feel it should be more.

CLAUD (*rising*) Then look at me, my friend, and save yourself some of the money you're not going to get.

ANDREA (*a little acidly*) There's no need to keep on telling him that, Claud. It sounds awfully good, I know, but . . . (*She breaks off*)

CLAUD. Keep on telling him what?

ANDREA. That he's not going to get anything.

CLAUD (*crossing to R of Andrea*) But I like telling him he's not going to get anything.

ANDREA. I dare say you do. It's not very flattering to me, though, is it?

CLAUD. Why not?

ANDREA. Well, it sounds as if you'd rather let me go altogether.

DUDLEY (*reasonably*) You know you'll have to pay me in the end, old man, so what's the sense in . . . ?

CLAUD (*interrupting*) Now look. Once and for all—I'm *not* going to pay you.

(ANDREA's *expression begins to harden*)

DUDLEY (*crossing to L of Andrea; incredulously*) You didn't expect me to let you have her for nothing, did you?

CLAUD. Well, certainly. It never occurred to me.

DUDLEY. What didn't?

CLAUD. All this under-the-counter business.

DUDLEY. But how should I manage, old man? I've nothing of my own. I've never earned a penny in my life. I mean, how am I going to *live*?

CLAUD. I see not the slightest need for you to live.

DUDLEY. Look. I'll make it nine thousand, seven hundred and fifty. How will that do?

CLAUD. Can't you get it into your head, you parasite? It isn't a question of haggling. I'm not interested.

(DUDLEY *shrugs, crosses to the armchair down L and sits*)

ANDREA (*staring at Claud; coldly*) I see. I'm sorry. I didn't realize.

CLAUD. What didn't you realize?

ANDREA (*loudly*) You don't think I'm worth nine thousand, seven hundred and fifty.

CLAUD. Of course I think you're worth nine thousand, seven hundred and fifty. That's nothing to do with it. One doesn't pay anything for a wife.

ANDREA. Oh, you would have accepted me as a gift, then?

CLAUD. Well, naturally, I . . .

ANDREA (*interrupting*) But, not if I *cost* anything.

CLAUD (*loudly*) Not if you cost *anything*.

ANDREA. Right. Well, at least you're honest about it. (*She turns and crosses angrily to the staircase*) I don't mind thrift, Claud, but if there's one thing I can't stand, it's a mean man.

(ANDREA *exits up the stairs.* DUDLEY *rises, scoops up Claud's hat, umbrella and brief-case from the floor, crosses with them and holds them out to Claud*)

CLAUD. What's the idea?

DUDLEY (*indicating the staircase*) Something tells me, old man . . .

Claud's bag of golf-clubs descends the staircase with a crash, and the shooting-stick, suitcase, camera-case, kitbag, tennis racquet, dressing-case, fishing-rod and small suitcase follow in rapid succession as—

the CURTAIN *falls*

ACT III

SCENE I

SCENE—*The same. Wednesday afternoon, before tea.*

When the CURTAIN *rises, there is brilliant sunshine. A bathing costume and towel are drying over the back of a chair on the sun-deck. The kitchen door is open and the room is filled with the strident blaring of a military band from the radio.* MRS O'CONNOR *is on the sun-deck transferring tea things from a tray to the table. The front door is heard to slam off.* ANDREA *enters hurriedly by the passage up* L. *She is attractively dressed for a sunny day. She crosses to the telephone, lifts the receiver and dials once. With some diffidence, she gently closes the kitchen door. The music ceases.*

ANDREA (*into the telephone*) Atlee four-six-four-seven, please. (*She waits*) Oh, Miss Winters, I'm so sorry, but it's me again. He wasn't on that one. Are you sure he said he was coming by train? . . . Oh, well I'll meet the next. You—er—you did give him my message? . . . Did he seem pleased? . . . Yes, it is difficult to tell with him, isn't it? Well, thank you so much, Miss Winters. I'll try not to bother you again. How are you keeping—all right? . . . That's right. Good-bye. (*She replaces the receiver and opens the kitchen door*)

(*The radio music blares forth*)

(*She puts her head into the kitchen and calls loudly*) Oh! Excuse me. Can you tell me what time the——

(*The music stops*)

(*at the top of her voice*) —next train gets in?

(*The just audible rumbling of a male voice is heard, off*)

Oh! Then is there a time-table, do you know?

(*The rumble is repeated*)

Oh—in the library. Thank you so much.

(ANDREA, *leaving the kitchen door open, moves down* L *and exits into the library. The music starts again.*

MRS O'CONNOR, *bringing the tray with her, comes into the room and crosses to the foot of the staircase.*

MISS BRIGGS *and* RON *enter on the sun-deck from* L. BRIGGS *is slim, pretty, eager, and very young. She wears a beret, skirt, jersey and sandals. Slung over her shoulder is a satchel.* Ron, *equally callow, is gangling, untidy, amiable, loutish and not very bright. He wears dirty grey flannel bags, a pullover, open-necked shirt, no hat and has a wild crop of hair. He carries an alarming-looking camera with a flash-bulb attachment, and slung from his shoulder is a leather case. He chews gum. They enter very tentatively, yet with an air of suppressed excitement)*

Mrs O'Connor *(calling up the stairs)* Your tea's ready. *(She listens for a reply, fails to hear one, then moves to the kitchen door and closes it)*

(The music ceases. Briggs *stands in the open french windows)*

(She returns to the stairs and calls) I say, the tea's getting cold.
Gertrude *(off upstairs)* Oh, thank you, Mrs er—um!
Mrs O'Connor *(to herself; bitterly)* "Mrs er—um!" *(She moves to the kitchen door)*

*(*Briggs *taps on the window jamb)*

(She turns. Inhospitably) Yes?
Briggs *(stepping into the room; timidly)* Oh—excuse me. I'm from *The Sun.*

*(*Ron *remains on the sun-deck)*

Mrs O'Connor *(slightly startled)* Where?
Briggs *(nervously)* I—I'm a reporter.
Mrs O'Connor. Oh! *(She crosses up* c) What is it you want?
Briggs. Is there a Mrs Nightshade here, please?
Mrs O'Connor. Not that *I* know of.
Briggs *(nonplussed)* Oh!

*(*Briggs *exchanges an anxious glance with* Ron)

Isn't this Mrs Fish's house?
Mrs O'Connor. Certainly it is. There's no Mrs Nightshade, though. There's a *Mr* Nightshade—off and on—and a Mrs Merrilees, but nothing in between. Why do you want to know?
Briggs *(crossing to* r *of Mrs O'Connor)* Well, you see, Mrs Fish is a friend of my mother's, and she knows that I'm just sort of— starting to be a reporter, and she's terribly kind, and she rang up my mother to say that this Mrs Nightshade had—had got a story that—that might do me a bit of good.
Mrs O'Connor. And she said you'd find her here?
Briggs. Yes.
Mrs O'Connor *(resignedly)* Well, of course, you may do, by now, for all I know. Nobody ever troubles to tell me who's staying here. *(She turns to go, then pauses)* Though, if you ask me—if it's something for the newspapers—it's Mrs Merrilees you want.

BRIGGS (*eagerly*) Is she in, please?

MRS O'CONNOR (*pessimistically*) She'll be coming in, I suppose, some time or other, for her tea.

BRIGGS. May we wait?

MRS O'CONNOR. Please yourself, my girl. (*She moves to the kitchen door*) People come and go as they like in this place.

(MRS O'CONNOR *exits to the kitchen. There is a brief burst of music as the door opens and closes.* BRIGGS *turns away, starts slightly at the burst of music, then motions to Ron to join her. She then crosses and sits on the left end of the window seat.* RON *moves warily to* L *of Briggs, where he stands chewing watchfully. Both seem very over-awed. There is a slight pause.*

GERTRUDE *enters down the stairs. She carries her bag.* BRIGGS *rises*)

GERTRUDE (*moving below the sofa; smiling vaguely*) How do you do?

BRIGGS. How do you do?

(GERTRUDE *sits on the sofa at the left end, takes a writing-pad and fountain pen from her bag, and begins to write*)

(*She glances uncertainly at Ron, then crosses to* C. *To Gertrude*) Excuse me.

(*There is no reply.* BRIGGS, *disconcerted, turns and holds a hurried, whispered conference with* RON)

GERTRUDE (*looking up and switching on*) Have you come to tea?

BRIGGS. No, thank you. No, I . . .

GERTRUDE (*interrupting*) Oh! (*She switches off and goes on writing*)

(BRIGGS *glances at Ron, then moves determinedly to Gertrude.* RON *edges to* R *of the table* R. GERTRUDE *switches on and looks up enquiringly*)

BRIGGS. Excuse me—but are you Mrs Merrilees?

GERTRUDE. Oh no, dear—I'm Miss Pigeon.

BRIGGS. Oh—I'm so sorry. (*She crosses to the left end of the window seat and sits*)

(GERTRUDE *switches off and goes on writing.* RON *sits carefully on the right end of the window seat.* BRIGGS *takes a notebook and pencil from her satchel and makes an entry in the book*)

GERTRUDE (*switching on*) Are you waiting for someone?

(BRIGGS *and* RON *rise*)

BRIGGS (*crossing to* C) Mrs Merrilees—I think.

GERTRUDE. Oh! But she's not Mrs Merrilees now, you know.

BRIGGS (*dismayed*) Isn't she?

GERTRUDE. No—she thought she was, but there's been a

muddle and she finds she isn't. (*She looks suddenly puzzled*) I don't quite know what she is now. She didn't say.

BRIGGS. Oh!

GERTRUDE (*thinking it over*) I do know that she doesn't intend to call herself by her first husband's name—so I suppose she must be going back to Mrs St John Willoughby—which is what she was in between. (*She switches off and goes on writing*)

BRIGGS (*completely bewildered*) Oh! Thank you. (*She crosses and sits on the left end of the window seat, then makes a note in her book*)

(RON *slowly resumes his seat.*

ANDREA *enters from the library down* L. *She is studying a time-table.* BRIGGS *and* RON *immediately jump to their feet*)

ANDREA (*looking up*) Oh—good afternoon. (*She crosses to* C)

BRIGGS (*with a step towards Andrea*) Good afternoon. I'm Briggs, of *The Sun.*

ANDREA. Oh, yes.

BRIGGS (*with a nervous rush of words*) Well, I'm not exactly *on The Sun*; I'm just a sort of local correspondent, and Mrs Fish was kind enough . . .

ANDREA (*holding out her hand*) I know. She telephoned me about you.

BRIGGS (*shaking hands*) Oh, she did. Oh, you *are* the lady.

ANDREA (*extending her hand to Ron*) How do you do?

RON (*shaking hands with Andrea*) Hiya!

ANDREA (*indicating the sofa*) Well, do come and sit down, er—Briggs. I shall be delighted to give you an "exclusive".

BRIGGS (*crossing to the sofa; breathless with excitement*) Oh, thank you. (*She sits on the sofa at the right end and opens her notebook*) Ei—*is it* Mrs St John Willoughby?

(RON *sits on the left end of the window seat*)

ANDREA (*standing* C) Oh, no, dear. That was the name I took to conceal my identity. There's no need for that any more.

BRIGGS. Oh! (*She hesitates with pencil poised*) I—don't quite know what to call you, then.

ANDREA. Well, strictly, of course, I'm Mrs Nightshade . . .

BRIGGS (*relieved*) Oh, you are. (*She makes a note*)

ANDREA. But I don't propose to be called that, because that would be unkind to Mr Merrilees. (*She considers*) Perhaps you'd better use my maiden name for the time being. There seems to be nothing else left.

BRIGGS. What is that, please?

ANDREA. Miss Pigeon.

BRIGGS. Oh! (*She glances in a confused way at Gertrude and makes a note*) And is it true, Miss Pigeon, that you are a rather notorious pers—I—I mean a rather famous person who was supposed to have—have murdered . . . ? (*She breaks off with a nervous little laugh*)

ANDREA. Yes. (*In mild surprise*) Didn't you know about it?

BRIGGS (*apologetically*) I'm sorry. I was at school.

ANDREA. Oh!

BRIGGS. They didn't let us read that sort of thing.

ANDREA. No—of course not.

BRIGGS. And now he's turned up again?

ANDREA. Yes.

BRIGGS. And—what does that mean, Miss Pigeon?

ANDREA (*crossing to* L *of the sofa*) Well, that means, you see, that if Mr Merrilees and I want to stay married—which we never really were, of course—I shall now have to get a divorce and be married again, although it was only on Monday that we *were* married.

BRIGGS (*frantically trying to make notes; looking up in agitated bewilderment*) I—er—I don't think I quite . . .

ANDREA. Because Dudley and I . . .

GERTRUDE (*suddenly looking up and switching on*) Did you say something, dear?

ANDREA. No, darling.

(GERTRUDE *switches off and goes on writing*)

(*Moving to the library door*) Perhaps we'd better go in here. (*She opens the door*)

(RON *rises*)

BRIGGS (*rising and moving to the library door*) Please, Miss Pigeon—who's Dudley—Mr Merrilees?

ANDREA. No, dear, Mr Nightshade. Though he's not really Dudley at all. He's Roderick.

(BRIGGS, *looking thoroughly confused, exits into the library*)

(*As she exits*) I only call him Dudley because . . .

(ANDREA *exits to the library, closing the door behind her.* RON, *looking more uncomfortable than ever, resumes his seat.*

DUDLEY *enters on the sun-deck from* L. *He wears an altogether more summery outfit, sports jacket, scarf, slacks and piebald shoes. He enters the room and crosses to* L, *registering considerable curiosity at the presence of* RON, *who rises slowly and returns* DUDLEY'S *gaze with a sort of trapped look.* DUDLEY *stands* L *of the sofa, bends over Gertrude, switches on her apparatus and kisses her.* GERTRUDE, *in pleased surprise, reaches round and pats Dudley's face*)

GERTRUDE. Oh—Dudley!

DUDLEY. Hullo, darling. Having a nice time?

GERTRUDE. Lovely, dear, lovely. I didn't know you were coming today.

DUDLEY. Andrea sent for me.

GERTRUDE. Oh!

(RON *slowly resumes his seat*)

DUDLEY. You don't know what she wants me for, I suppose?
GERTRUDE. No, dear. (*She ponders*) Unless it's to put a new flint in her lighter. She did say it needed one. (*She beckons*)

(DUDLEY *moves close to Gertrude*)

(*Confidentially*) I don't think that Mr O'Connor's very good with his hands, you know.
DUDLEY. No.

(BRIGGS *enters from the library. Remaining in the doorway, she jerks her head at Ron, then sees Dudley*)

BRIGGS. Oh! Excuse me.

(BRIGGS *exits to the library.*
    RON *rises with alacrity, and rushes across to the library door, almost collides with Dudley, then exits into the library*)

DUDLEY (*startled*) Who are they?
GERTRUDE. I don't know, dear.
DUDLEY (*indicating the library*) Is Andrea with them?
GERTRUDE (*looking vaguely around the room*) I suppose she must be. She was here just now.

(DUDLEY *moves to the library door and stands listening*)

Is that all, then, for the moment?
DUDLEY (*moving above the sofa*) Yes, dear. You get on with your letter.
GERTRUDE. Yes. (*She switches off, takes a stamped envelope from her bag, and addresses it*)

(DUDLEY *soliloquizes, but leans over Gertrude as if talking to her*)

DUDLEY. Now, why did she send for me—huh? It can't be that she's decided she wants me back, can it? Or, can it? It might be, you know—if only to annoy him. The thing is, though—what do I do if it is that? Do I have her and risk it—or what? I'm damned if I know. (*He moves below the sofa, sits on it R of Gertrude, and attracts her attention*)

(GERTRUDE *switches on*)

I'm sorry to disturb you again.
GERTRUDE. Oh, it isn't that, dear. (*She indicates the bag*) My high tension's getting a little low, that's all.
DUDLEY. I won't keep you.
GERTRUDE. Well?
DUDLEY. Aunt Gertrude—you know Andrea, don't you?

GERTRUDE (*puzzled*) Know her, dear? Of course I do. What are you talking about?

DUDLEY. I mean, you know her very well—better than anyone, perhaps?

GERTRUDE (*thoughtfully*) I think, perhaps, I do—now that dear Maggie is gone. She lived with her, of course.

DUDLEY (*after a slight spasm of anxiety*) Yes. Well, *you* never doubted her, did you? At the trial, I mean.

GERTRUDE. At the trial, dear? Why should I? It was all stuff and nonsense—especially that young woman who said she saw her do it.

DUDLEY (*earnestly*) You just knew she wouldn't do a thing like that?

GERTRUDE (*scornfully*) With somebody looking on? Of course not. She has far too much sense.

DUDLEY. But apart from that, I mean—didn't you feel that she was—well, too essentially kind to—to kill anyone?

GERTRUDE (*patting Dudley's knee*) My dear—I've known Andrea draw blood from the head of an under-gardener with a hoe—simply because he drowned a half-grown rat in the water-butt. Now if that doesn't show an essential kindness, I don't know what does.

DUDLEY (*as if surprised at his own reaction*) I *do* know what you mean by that.

GERTRUDE. And that was when she was only ten. So she's not very likely to drown a full-sized man in an ocean at the age of thirty-two herself, is she?

DUDLEY (*reassured*) No.

GERTRUDE. You know how fond I am of you, dear.

(DUDLEY *smiles and lays a hand on hers*)

Well, you don't think I should have gone on leaving my money to her if I had thought she'd pushed *you* in the sea, surely?

(DUDLEY *pricks up his ears*)

Why, she would never have seemed the same to me again.

DUDLEY (*trying to sound offhand*) Oh—you've left her your money. I didn't know.

GERTRUDE. Indeed I have. All of it—now. I wrote and told them so.

DUDLEY. Who, dear?

GERTRUDE. The Government. I was going to let them have some of it, because they seemed so worried about money. But after treating Andrea like that . . .

DUDLEY. I should think so, indeed.

GERTRUDE. And not a word of apology, mind you—even when they had to let her go. (*Suddenly perplexed*) But why do you keep on asking me that?

Dudley (*blankly*) What?

Gertrude. Whether I doubted her, dear.

Dudley. I haven't asked you before.

Gertrude. Haven't you? Are you sure?

Dudley. Certain.

Gertrude (*thoughtfully*) Ah, yes—now I remember. It was Mr Merrilees—yesterday—before he left. (*Puzzled*) But why should you ask me at all? It seems such a funny question for *you* to ask. You don't think she murdered him, do you?

Dudley. Murdered who?

Gertrude. Oh, but of course it was you, wasn't it? Yes—I must get on. (*She switches off and sticks down the envelope*)

(Dudley, *looking thoughtful, rises and moves to* R *of the sofa*)

(*She switches on*) By the way—you're not going to let him have her, are you?

Dudley (*moving above the sofa and leaning over the back*) Do you know, dear—I don't think I am.

Gertrude. That's right. (*She pats his hand, rises and moves up* L) I must take this to the post.

Dudley. I'll do that for you.

Gertrude. Oh, will you? You are kind. (*She hands Dudley the letter*)

Dudley. Which way's the box?

Gertrude. It's—um—let me see. Well, I'll come with you, dear, shall I, and show you? I'll get my hat.

(Gertrude *exits up the stairs.* Dudley *puts the letter in his pocket, smiles indulgently and wanders down* C.

Andrea, Briggs *and* Ron *enter from the library.* Andrea *crosses to* L *of Dudley.* Briggs *and* Ron *remain down* L)

Andrea. Oh, here is Mr Nightshade now. Dudley dear, this is Briggs—a little friend of Valerie's who's on *The Sun.*

Dudley (*politely impressed*) Indeed. (*He bows slightly*)

Briggs. How do you do?

Andrea (*indicating Ron*) And Mr—um . . .

Ron (*lifting his arm*) Hiya!

(Dudley *lifts his arm to Ron*)

Andrea. I've given her an interview and had my picture taken looking at my two marriage certificates. Actually they were old dog licences belonging to Valerie, but they were all we could find and it won't show. Good evening, dear. (*She presents her cheek to him*)

Dudley (*kissing Andrea*) Hullo, darling. (*He puts an arm around her shoulders*)

Briggs (*to Andrea; in a state of anxious confusion*) Excuse me—I—

I'm terribly sorry—but still haven't got it quite clear. (*She indicates Dudley*) Is this the gentleman you've just married?

DUDLEY (*all charm and affability*) No. I'm the one who went in the sea.

BRIGGS (*crossing to Dudley; excitedly*) Oh! Oh, I wonder whether . . . Oh, could I persuade you to . . . ?

DUDLEY (*interrupting*) Make a statement? Of course. I should be delighted. What would you like me to tell you about?

BRIGGS. Oh, anything, Mr Nightshade, anything, but—but . . . (*She breaks off*)

DUDLEY (*encouragingly*) Yes?

BRIGGS. Well, if you could say something about—how you *got* in the sea.

DUDLEY. Certainly. (*He ponders for a moment*)

(BRIGGS *perches herself on the right arm of the sofa, and opens her notebook*)

(*He disengages himself from Andrea and wanders down* R) You can say this—and quote me. (*He dictates*) I returned to this country a few weeks ago—after having lain for nine months—in an African—— (*he hesitates and glances fleetingly at Andrea*)

(BRIGGS *scribbles madly*)

—hospital—with amnesia.

BRIGGS (*looking up; startled*) Who did you say?

DUDLEY. Loss of memory.

BRIGGS. Oh! (*She writes*)

DUDLEY (*crossing to* R *of Andrea*) At first I was unable to establish contact with my wife. When finally I did so—I was shocked and astonished to learn—that, in my absence—she had been charged with my death. The allegation—that she pushed me in the sea—is, of course—(*he puts his arm about Andrea and smiles at her*) the foulest calumny.

ANDREA (*deeply appreciative*) Dudley. How nice of you.

BRIGGS (*holding up her hand like a schoolgirl*) Please.

DUDLEY. Yes?

BRIGGS. What's cal-calumn . . . ?

DUDLEY. A calumny, Briggs, is a false and malicious accusation. A defamation—a slander. She fought like a wild thing to *save* my life.

ANDREA. Oh, you can do the sweetest and most unexpected things, Dudley.

DUDLEY (*to Briggs; smugly*) Will that do?

BRIGGS (*scribbling*) Oh—boy!

DUDLEY (*removing his arm from Andrea*) Now—would you like a picture?

BRIGGS (*rising and putting her notebook in the satchel*) Oh, please.

DUDLEY (*considering*) Well . . . (*He takes* ANDREA's *arm and leads*

E

her down L) What about my wife in the chair—(*he thrusts* ANDREA *into the armchair down* L) and me on the arm—(*he perches himself on the upstage arm of the chair and puts his arm about Andrea*) like this?

(RON, *suddenly electrified at the prospect of a picture, crosses quickly to* LC, *turns, crouches and assesses the group*)

BRIGGS. Wonderful—eh, Ron?
RON. Smashin'.
ANDREA (*suddenly rising and moving below the sofa*) No—I don't think so, Dudley, if you don't mind.

(BRIGGS *and* RON *look dismayed*)

DUDLEY (*startled*) Not?
ANDREA. Not without Claud, dear. It wouldn't be in very good taste.
DUDLEY (*rising; resentfully*) What do you mean? I'm your husband.

(RON, *the picture of resentful disappointment, straightens up*)

ANDREA. Only on paper, though. Don't lose sight of that.
DUDLEY (*aggressively*) I've every intention of . . .
ANDREA (*to Briggs; interrupting*) So if you wouldn't mind waiting a little while . . . ?
BRIGGS. Not at all.

(DUDLEY *moves huffily up* C)

ANDREA (*to Ron; consolingly*) Then they can both be in it.
BRIGGS. Yes.
ANDREA (*crossing and opening the library door*) Then perhaps you'd go back in here, dear, would you?
BRIGGS (*crossing to* L) Certainly.

(RON *crosses sullenly to* L)

ANDREA. I want to talk to Mr Nightshade before Mr Merrilees gets here.

(BRIGGS *and* RON *exit to the library.* ANDREA *closes the door, then turns and looks thoughtfully at Dudley*)

DUDLEY (*moving down* C; *not too pleased*) You've sent for *him*, then, have you?
ANDREA. Yes.
DUDLEY. What for?
ANDREA. Because I want to tell him how deeply ashamed of myself I am.
DUDLEY. Ashamed—why?
ANDREA. For being angry with him for showing the very qualities for which I married him.

Dudley (*scornfully*) You're referring, I take it, to his rather marked integrity, honour and—what have you?

Andrea. Yes, dear. His integrity, honour and what you haven't. (*She moves to the armchair down* L)

Dudley (*acidly*) Why trouble to send for me, then?

Andrea. To take up your offer, Dudley. (*She sits*)

Dudley (*astonished*) What?

Andrea. The one you made to him.

Dudley. Pay the ten thousand yourself, you mean?

Andrea. Nine thousand, seven hundred and fifty—to be exact.

Dudley (*impressed*) Well—you do want him, don't you?

Andrea. I do.

Dudley. He wouldn't have been worth all that to you this time last week, however.

Andrea (*ironically intrigued*) He wouldn't?

Dudley. No. It's a good thing I realize that—otherwise I might be hurt.

Andrea. What's happened in the meantime then—to make him seem less worthless?

Dudley. *I've* come back.

Andrea. Ah, yes. I do see that.

Dudley (*undismayed*) You have a use for him now?

Andrea. Hadn't I a use for him before?

Dudley. Only as a moral soporific.

Andrea. And what has he become, since you came back?

Dudley (*crossing to Andrea*) Something in the nature of a sanctuary, dear.

Andrea. A what?

Dudley. A haven, a harbour, a port in a storm.

Andrea. What storm?

Dudley (*leaning over her and pointing to his chest*) Me.

Andrea (*flattening herself against the back of the chair*) Have you any idea what you're talking about?

Dudley. I am talking about your constitutional inability to resist me, Andrea.

Andrea (*falsely incredulous*) My *what*!

Dudley. Which is better known to you than anyone. So don't pretend you don't know what I mean.

Andrea (*blustering*) Are you suggesting . . . ?

Dudley (*interrupting and leaning closer*) Yes. So long as you're free to return to me—I have only to do that—(*he snaps his fingers*) and you will.

Andrea (*staring unbelievingly at him*) Return to you!

Dudley. Willy-nilly! Against your better judgement. Whether you like it or not. (*He straightens up*)

Andrea (*rising and escaping from the chair*) You're demented. (*She moves away* R, *trying not to hurry*)

DUDLEY (*moving slowly after Andrea*) You have no defences where I'm concerned—and you know it.

ANDREA. That's nonsense! (*She realizes he is following her, so she turns defensively and backs away as he advances*)

DUDLEY. You're helpless—and you know you're helpless.

ANDREA (*brought to a halt by the armchair down* R) Well, you keep away, because . . .

DUDLEY (*interrupting and moving close to Andrea*) I have only to touch you . . . (*He deliberately takes her in his arms*)

ANDREA (*leaning away from him; sharply*) Dudley!

DUDLEY (*drawing her to him*) And you're sunk.

ANDREA. *Dud*ley!

(DUDLEY *kisses her. At first,* ANDREA *resists, then, by degrees, the kiss becomes mutual*)

DUDLEY (*as their lips part*) See?

ANDREA (*very shaken*) What do you think you're doing?

DUDLEY (*still holding her*) Demonstrating, dear, that's all.

ANDREA (*pushing herself away from him and crossing to* C) Well, stop demonstrating and get down to business. I—I've got a train to meet.

DUDLEY (*crossing to* R *of Andrea; leering*) I *am* getting down to business.

ANDREA. Oh, I see. Pushing the price up. All right, I'll make it eleven thousand.

(DUDLEY *shakes his head, and begins again to take her in his arms*)

(*The right end of the sofa prevents her backing away*) Twelve, then.

(*Again he kisses her. Again she responds*)

(*The fight gone out of her; remaining with her arms about his neck. Anxiously*) You don't mean that you do want me back, though, do you—not really?

DUDLEY. I do want you back.

ANDREA (*with growing dismay*) But, Dudley, we're a terrible mixture. You must be joking.

DUDLEY. Do I seem to be joking?

ANDREA (*wailing*) No.

DUDLEY (*gently*) I'll try to do better, this time, dear.

ANDREA. Oh, but I do so want to live in peace—with someone I can respect, Dudley.

(DUDLEY'S *expression hardens*)

(*Imploringly*) Dudley—please—if you've the slightest regard for my happiness. He's so much nicer than you are.

(DUDLEY *removes Andrea's arms from about his neck and crosses down* L)

Thirteen thousand.

DUDLEY (*loudly*) No.

ANDREA. But, Dudley . . .

DUDLEY. You're not for sale. (*He grabs a woman's magazine from the coffee table and sits on the sofa*)

ANDREA. But, yesterday you said . . .

DUDLEY (*interrupting*) I've changed my mind. (*He opens the magazine*)

(ANDREA *stares helplessly at Dudley for a moment, then suddenly stamps with anger*)

ANDREA. Well, I'm not going to have it, that's all. (*She paces up* R *and turns*) It isn't fair, using your beastly charm like that. It—it's blackmail—that's what it is. (*She paces to* R *of the sofa*) Why have you changed your mind, anyway?

DUDLEY (*doubtfully*) Because—well, because I . . .

ANDREA (*interrupting*) That, of course, I don't believe.

DUDLEY (*looking at the magazine*) As you please.

ANDREA (*moving up* L) Something's convinced you that I'm worth keeping, that's all. (*She pauses and thinks*)

(DUDLEY *maintains a discreet silence*)

Either you've discovered that I'm richer than you thought, or you've managed to satisfy yourself that I didn't push you in the sea—or something. (*She pauses. Suddenly her look of resentment gives place to one of mischief. She moves above the sofa and leans over Dudley*) Well, as a matter of fact—and if you really want to know—I *did*.

DUDLEY. Did what?

ANDREA. Push you in the sea. And you can put that in your pipe and . . .

(DUDLEY *grins*)

Now what are you grinning at?

DUDLEY (*smiling in a superior way*) Really, Andrea.

ANDREA (*straightening up*) Oh—I suppose you think I'm just saying that.

DUDLEY. You're slipping, my poppet. (*He turns a page*)

ANDREA. All right. So you think I'm just trying to scare you off. (*She leans over Dudley and puts her mouth close to his ear. Evilly insinuating*) You can't be sure, though, can you—not *quite* sure?

DUDLEY (*amused*) I'm reasonably so.

ANDREA (*trying to look like "Mr Hyde"*) Are you? Why? Why even reasonably sure? Because you wouldn't expect me to do such a thing? We don't all look like it, you know. Babyface Nelson, for instance.

(DUDLEY *looks at Andrea and the grin leaves his face*)

DUDLEY. Well—it's a risk I'm prepared to take, anyway.

ANDREA. Very well. (*She moves up* R) But I should think twice before thwarting a woman of my reputation. You don't get all that smoke without some fire, Dudley.

DUDLEY (*with a look of disquiet in his eyes*) That, of course, like most proverbs, is a complete fallacy.

ANDREA. Well—so long as you're happy about it. (*She goes on to the sun-deck, returns and points to the magazine Dudley is reading*) I shouldn't start reading any serials, though.

(ANDREA *exits on the sun-deck to* L. DUDLEY, *with a look of alarm, rises and tosses the magazine on to the coffee table.*

ANDREA *re-enters and stands in the open french windows*)

(*With a sinister air*) I spoke to Valerie this morning.

DUDLEY. Uh?

ANDREA. *She* told me something you might care to ponder, too.

DUDLEY. Oh?

ANDREA. Yes. If you're tried for something, and you get let off—you can't be charged again—not with the same offence. Did you know that?

DUDLEY. What about it?

ANDREA. Well—I have been tried for murdering you once, haven't I?

(ANDREA *exits on the sun-deck to* L. DUDLEY, *looking shaken, crosses down* L.

MRS O'CONNOR *enters from the kitchen. There is a burst of music as the door opens and closes.* DUDLEY *sits in the armchair down* L. MRS O'CONNOR *crosses to the french windows, looks at the tea-table, turns, rolls her eyes to heaven and crosses to the kitchen door. There is a knock at the front door off.*

MRS O'CONNOR *registers suffering and exits by the passage up* L. DUDLEY, *becoming aware of something uncomfortable in his chair, scrabbles a moment behind him and produces a book.*

CLAUD *enters by the passage. He wears a black coat and pin-stripe trousers. He carries a newspaper in addition to his bowler, brief-case and umbrella.* DUDLEY *looks at the title of the book and reacts*)

DUDLEY. Good God!

CLAUD (*crossing to the sideboard*) Good evening. (*He puts his umbrella on the sideboard, then crosses to the left end of the window seat, puts his hat and brief-case on the table* R *and sits. He puts on his spectacles and opens the newspaper*)

(MRS O'CONNOR *enters by the passage*)

DUDLEY (*rising and moving up* L; *to Mrs O'Connor*) I say.

(MRS O'CONNOR *stops by the kitchen door and looks bleakly at Dudley*)

(*He indicates the book*) Who's reading this—d'you know?

Mrs O'Connor. I have no idea what goes on in this house, Mr Nightshade.

    (Mrs O'Connor *glances at Claud, then exits to the kitchen. As she does so, there is the usual burst of music*)

Dudley (*crossing to Claud*) It isn't yours, I suppose?

Claud (*looking up; frigidly*) What isn't mine?

Dudley (*indicating the book*) *The Crimes of the Borgias.*

Claud. She brought it with her—on her honeymoon.

Dudley. Oh!

Claud. She likes to read in bed, I understand.

Dudley. Did she seem to enjoy it?

Claud (*angrily*) How the hell should I know? (*He retires behind his paper*)

    (Dudley *stares sullenly at Claud, moves down* l *and throws the book on to the armchair*)

Dudley. Why didn't you let me know you were coming? You could have driven down with me.

Claud. Thank you, but I prefer the wholesome squalor of British Railways. (*He lowers his paper and looks at Dudley*) And before you make any further effort to be friendly, I may tell you that I'm fully aware you were lying when you said you could remember whether Andrea pushed you in the sea. (*He goes on reading*)

Dudley. Oh! (*He pauses*) Well, look! D'you mind if I ask you something?

Claud. The point is, of course, academic. You will ask me in any case. (*He gives Dudley his attention*) Well?

Dudley (*moving to* l *of Claud; worried*) Well, you know the law about being tried twice for the same offence. You can't be; you know that, don't you?

Claud. Not once you've been acquitted, of course.

Dudley. Quite. Well, Andrea's got hold of that, and she seems to think it means she could bump me off, now, any time she liked, and nobody could do a thing about it.

Claud (*with a short laugh*) Ingenious, anyway. (*He continues with his paper*)

Dudley (*moving down* r; *anxiously seeking reassurance*) That can't be right, though, surely? It wouldn't be the same offence if she did it again. (*He turns*) Would it?

Claud. Hardly an offence at all, in my view.

Dudley. No, seriously . . .

Claud. Andrea has a genius for misinterpreting the law. We know that. I don't know what comfort it would be, though, with a knife in your back, to reflect that it got there illegally.

Dudley (*glaring at Claud*) You sweet thing! (*He moves up* c)

CLAUD (*looking up*) From all of which I take it that you are planning to live with her again.

DUDLEY. Well, as a matter of fact, I am—though I'm damned if I know what I've said to suggest it.

CLAUD. A certain concern for your personal safety suggests it. (*He continues with his paper*)

DUDLEY. You're just plain, bloody callous, of course. You don't seem to think it matters.

CLAUD. I can see that it matters to you.

DUDLEY. Doesn't it matter to you, too? I thought you didn't like women who went in for that sort of thing.

CLAUD. I don't.

DUDLEY (*alarmed*) You don't mean you're dropping out, do you?

CLAUD (*looking up; surprised*) Would you mind?

DUDLEY. Well, of course I'd mind if it meant you didn't believe in her. If I'm going to have her back, I shall need all the moral support I can get. (*He crosses to* L)

CLAUD (*returning to his paper*) Well—if it's any comfort to you—I'm not dropping out.

DUDLEY (*relieved*) Ah! You do believe in her, then. (*He perches himself on the left arm of the sofa*)

CLAUD. Not yet. Not implicitly—no.

DUDLEY (*startled*) Uh?

CLAUD. I do know how to find out about her though.

DUDLEY (*rising*) What? (*He crosses hurriedly to Claud*) What did you say?

CLAUD (*looking up*) I said—"I do know how to find out about her, *though*". I've given the matter considerable thought and—(*deliberately*) I now know how to find out about her. Is that clear?

DUDLEY. I suppose it's not the least use asking you how?

(CLAUD *rises, removes his spectacles and thrusts his face close to Dudley's*)

CLAUD (*loudly*) Not the slightest.

DUDLEY (*furiously*) You know—I've been trying to like you, for Andrea's sake——

(*The front door is heard to slam off*)

—but, from now on, so help me . . .

(ANDREA *enters hurriedly from the passage up* L. DUDLEY, *fuming, moves* R *of the sofa.* CLAUD *puts his newspaper on the table* R *and picks up his brief-case*)

ANDREA (*running to Claud; delightedly*) Darling—you're here. (*She flings herself at him and ardently kisses him*) I missed you. You must have come the other way.

CLAUD (*stiffly*) Yes.

ANDREA. I'm so glad to see you. (*She kisses him*) I've been so wretched, waiting.

CLAUD. Wretched? Why?

ANDREA. Didn't they tell you? (*She indicates Dudley*) Didn't he tell you?

DUDLEY. What?

ANDREA. How sorry I am for throwing him out last night.

DUDLEY. No, I'm damned if I . . .

ANDREA (*interrupting*) Well, I do think you might have done, Dudley.

CLAUD (*sourly*) Oh, I got all that, all right—from Miss Winters.

ANDREA (*relieved*) Oh, you did!

CLAUD. *And* from the porter at the club.

ANDREA. And am I forgiven? (*She is still clinging to him*) Well, I must be, mustn't I—otherwise you wouldn't be here?

CLAUD. As a matter of fact, Andrea, I was coming anyway. (*He pats his brief-case*) I wanted to see you about something.

ANDREA. Oh!

(GERTRUDE *enters down the stairs. She wears her hat and carries the cricket bat*)

GERTRUDE (*to Dudley*) I'm ready, dear.

DUDLEY (*uncomprehendingly*) Huh?

GERTRUDE. Didn't you say you had to go to the post?

DUDLEY (*taking the letter from his pocket*) Oh—yes. (*He moves above the sofa*)

(GERTRUDE *turns to the passage up* L)

(*He indicates the bat*) What are you taking that for?

GERTRUDE (*stopping and turning*) What, dear? This? Oh, yes, I brought it down to do it up. I want to send it.

DUDLEY (*taking the bat from Gertrude*) Well, Claud's your man for that.

GERTRUDE. Is he?

DUDLEY (*crossing to Claud*) Certainly he is. He used to play for Kent. (*He hands the bat to Claud, then returns up* L)

GERTRUDE. Oh, well, that's lovely. (*To Claud. Graciously*) Thank you so much.

(GERTRUDE *and* DUDLEY *exit by the passage up* L)

ANDREA (*moving below the sofa; resentfully*) Honestly—I could murder that man sometimes. (*She sits on the sofa at the left end*)

CLAUD. Where is the paper and string, Andrea?

ANDREA. Oh, leave it for the moment, dear. (*She pats the seat of the sofa*) Let's talk while there's a little peace in the place.

(CLAUD *crosses to the sofa and sits* R *of Andrea with the bat and brief-case on his lap*)

(*She clings to Claud*) Darling, I want you to promise me something.

CLAUD. Yes?

ANDREA. In future, when I get mad with you for being honourable—you're to take no notice.

CLAUD (*perplexed*) Huh?

ANDREA. It isn't reasonable of me.

CLAUD. Isn't it?

ANDREA. No—particularly when you think that it's precisely for being what you are, that I married you.

CLAUD. What am I, then? I've rather forgotten.

ANDREA. Well—honourable, Claud.

CLAUD. Oh! (*He opens the brief-case*)

ANDREA. I'm apt to be unreasonable at times, you know.

CLAUD (*apparently surprised*) *Are* you?

ANDREA. Yes. You'll learn that when you get to know me better. Meanwhile, though—if you *could* just remember, when I do hit you, or throw things about, or anything . . .

CLAUD. To ignore it.

ANDREA. Please. Or I shall worry about you—you take things so seriously.

CLAUD. Very well. (*He puts on his spectacles*) I'll do what I can.

ANDREA. There's a dear. (*She sits up and looks business-like*) Now —what did you want to see me about?

CLAUD (*taking a large sheaf of papers from the brief-case and putting them on the coffee table*) This matter of bigamy, Andrea. (*He takes a single sheet from the brief-case*)

ANDREA (*blankly*) What matter of bigamy?

CLAUD (*staring at her*) Surely you must realize . . . ?

ANDREA. What?

CLAUD. Well, that—technically, my dear, you've committed . . .

ANDREA. I have?

CLAUD. Yes.

ANDREA (*astonished*) In marrying you, you mean?

CLAUD. Yes.

ANDREA (*pugnaciously*) Who says so?

CLAUD. Well, it's—it's obvious.

ANDREA (*rising*) What's obvious? I never heard such nonsense in my life. (*She grabs the sheaf of papers from the coffee table*) Have you been seeing that Sir Henry Thing again?

CLAUD. This morning.

ANDREA. Ah! I might have known.—How can it possibly be bigamy when I was a widow?

CLAUD. But you weren't a widow.

ANDREA. Then how could I have killed him?

CLAUD (*patiently*) You didn't kill him. That's why it's bigamy.

ANDREA. I see. So it's a crime to kill your husband, and it's a crime *not* to kill your husband. That makes sense, I must say. Really, Claud, it's too much. First it's murder, then it's bigamy. What'll it be next—mayhem or nepotism? (*She throws the papers high into the air so that they flutter down all around Claud*)

(CLAUD *waits until the last paper has floated to the floor*)

CLAUD. Is this the sort of thing I'm to ignore?

(ANDREA, *aghast at what she has done, stares at Claud*)

I was only going to relieve your mind about it, anyway. (*He puts the single paper into the brief-case*)

ANDREA (*hurriedly sitting L of Claud on the sofa*) Oh, I am so sorry. Oh, please go on and relieve my mind, darling.

(CLAUD *hesitates uncertainly*)

Please!

CLAUD (*taking the paper from his brief-case*) Very well. (*He reads*) "Mrs Nightshade would have been entitled to assume that all proper enquiries had been made to trace her husband before she was charged with his murder."

ANDREA (*surprised*) Did Sir Henry say that?

CLAUD. He did.

ANDREA. Perhaps I've misjudged him.

CLAUD (*reading*) "Thus—although the murder charge did not —for matrimonial purposes—create a legal presumption of Mr Nightshade's death, and Mrs Nightshade's second marriage was therefore bigamous . . ."

ANDREA (*sitting up; contentiously*) Now, look . . .

CLAUD (*interrupting sharply*) *Wait* a minute, will you? (*He glares at her*)

(ANDREA'S *fingers fly to her mouth as she recollects herself*)

(*He shakes the paper sternly and reads*) "It would, nevertheless, provide an answer to a charge of bigamy."

ANDREA. Oh!

CLAUD (*reading*) "And, this being so, I am confident that the Director of Public Prosecutions would be prepared to assure Mrs Nightshade that he will not authorize such a prosecution." (*He puts the paper on the coffee table, takes off his spectacles and puts them in his pocket*)

ANDREA. Well—that *is* nice.

(CLAUD, *with a suddenly preoccupied air, puts the brief-case on the coffee table, rises, and absently taking the bat with him, moves away*)

Dear Sir Henry. We must ask him to dinner some time. (*She leans back in the corner of the sofa and puts up her feet*)

CLAUD. Yes.

ANDREA. Anything else?

CLAUD (*standing with his back to her*) Yes—Dudley. I suggest that we kill him.

ANDREA (*sitting up; astonished*) What?

CLAUD. I see no alternative, Andrea. We are utterly in his power. And unless we are prepared to sacrifice everything—there's nothing else to be done. (*He pauses and seems to be listening for the effect of his words*)

(ANDREA, *expressionless, subsides and turns slowly to face the back of the sofa*)

I thought, perhaps—if we took him for a walk—along the cliff-tops—at night—or asked him to go for a swim with us, or . . .

(ANDREA *makes a muffled sound and her shoulders shake*)

(*He turns. Hurrying behind the sofa*) Andrea—you're crying. (*He leans over her*) Thank God, you're crying.

(ANDREA *turns and sits up. She is convulsed with laughter*)

ANDREA. Oh, Claud—you're wonderful!

CLAUD (*angrily astonished*) What the hell's funny about that?

ANDREA. What a way to find out what sort of a person I am. I never knew anyone so artless.

CLAUD (*shouting; furiously*) Blast you, Andrea. (*He flings away up* R) You are the most maddening creature.

ANDREA (*rising and crossing to Claud*) I'm sorry to laugh, dear, but if you'd only learn to trust me, this sort of thing wouldn't happen. What would you have done if I'd agreed? (*With renewed laughter, she attaches herself to his arm and drops her forehead on to his shoulder*)

(BRIGGS *enters from the library*)

BRIGGS (*peering enquiringly round the door*) Excuse me. Did any-one call?

(ANDREA *disengages herself from Claud, moves to* R *of the sofa and tries to recover her composure*)

ANDREA. Oh, I am sorry, Briggs. I forgot. (*To Claud*) This young lady's a reporter, dear. I promised her a picture. (*Exhausted with laughter*) Oh, dear! (*She dabs her eyes with her handkerchief*)

BRIGGS (*moving excitedly down* LC) Is this Mr Merrilees, then?

ANDREA. Yes. (*She looks at Claud and collapses with laughter*)

(RON *enters from the library and stands sheepishly and unobtrusively down* L)

BRIGGS (*going to Claud and taking her notebook from her satchel*) Oh, Mr Merrilees—would you care to make a statement?

CLAUD (*moving to* L *of the window seat; fiercely*) What about?

BRIGGS (*flustered*) About—about your—your plans—for—for the future.

CLAUD. What makes you think *I* plan my future? (*He sits on the left end of the window seat*)

(BRIGGS *retires in disorder up* C.

GERTRUDE *and* DUDLEY *enter by the passage up* L. DUDLEY *looks distastefully at Claud*)

GERTRUDE (*to Dudley*) Thank you, dear.

(GERTRUDE *exits up the stairs*)

ANDREA. Ah! Here's the other one. Come, Dudley.

(DUDLEY *remains sullenly up* L.)

(*She moves below the sofa. To Briggs*) Where would you like us—on this? (*She sits centre of the sofa and strikes a pose*)

(BRIGGS *moves eagerly down* RC. RON, *galvanized into action, rushes to* C *and crouches with his camera directed at Andrea.* BRIGGS *squats behind Ron*)

RON. Sooper! (*He prepares his camera*)
ANDREA. Come then, Dudley—Claud.

(CLAUD *rises. With ill grace both men mooch behind the sofa,* CLAUD *absently shouldering the cricket bat*)

(*To Ron*) How would you like us?
RON. Er—well—how about you two on the sofa holdin' hands, and the other . . .
ANDREA (*interrupting*) Which two?
RON (*surprised*) You and the legal one.

(DUDLEY *emits a short, aggravating laugh.* CLAUD *throws him an angry look*)

ANDREA (*to Dudley*) Ssh! (*To Ron. Encouragingly*) Yes, go on.
RON. 'N' the other feller leanin' over the back lookin' cheesed off?
BRIGGS (*enthusiastically*) Oh—wizard!
CLAUD (*glaring at Ron*) Listen, young man—if I consent to appear in the same picture at all with this—(*he indicates Dudley*) this spiv, I'm . . .

(DUDLEY *reacts and faces Claud*)

ANDREA (*interrupting sharply*) Claud!
DUDLEY (*to Claud; aggressively*) Look—I'm getting a little tired of you, you know, one way and another. I'm half inclined to . . .
ANDREA (*interrupting sharply*) Dudley. (*Sternly*) Come and sit down.

(DUDLEY, *muttering mutinously, moves below the sofa and sits on it,* L *of Andrea. He folds his arms, crosses his legs and turns away his head*)

(*To Claud*) Both of you.

(CLAUD *moves below the sofa, sits* R *of Andrea, with the bat across his lap, crosses his legs and turns away his head*)

(*In an undertone*) You ought to be ashamed of yourselves. (*She strikes a pose. To Ron*) There! How will that do? (*She puts on a smile*)

(BRIGGS *and* RON *doubtfully survey the group*)

RON (*plaintively*) Couldn't one of 'em put his arm round you, or something?

ANDREA (*doubtfully*) Well, I . . . (*She breaks off and glances at Claud*)

BRIGGS. And the other hold your hand—to make it fair?

DUDLEY (*to Briggs; uncrossing his arms and legs and sitting forward*) Let's get this clear, shall we? I'm the lady's husband. If there's anything like that to be done—I do all of it—see?

BRIGGS (*intimidated*) Yes, Mr Nightshade. (*She rises and backs down* R)

DUDLEY (*indicating Claud*) This person is nothing more than a rather doubtful boy-friend, and . . .

(CLAUD *reacts, uncrosses his legs and turns to face Dudley*)

ANDREA (*interrupting*) Be quiet, Dudley.

CLAUD (*bristling across Andrea*) May I say that I find that offensive?

ANDREA (*turning to Claud*) You be quiet, too.

DUDLEY (*truculently*) That's exactly what you're meant to find, and if you want to make something of it . . .

CLAUD (*rising and flourishing the bat; overlapping the previous speech from "find"*) In that case, perhaps you'd care to come outside and repeat it?

DUDLEY (*half rising*) Certainly, I'll . . .

ANDREA. Stop it—the pair of you.

(DUDLEY *and* CLAUD *subside and resume their seats, fuming*)

(*To Ron*) I think they'd better just sit, if you don't mind.

RON (*shrugging resignedly*) O.K. (*He crouches and focuses his camera*)

DUDLEY (*with averted head; muttering*) Let him get his damn picture, and I'll have the greatest pleasure in coming outside.

(RON *puts his camera on the floor, rises and crosses to Dudley*)

CLAUD. Good.

RON (*to Dudley*) Would you mind just . . . ? (*He seizes one of Dudley's legs and crosses it over the other*) That's right. Looks more cosy, see? (*He stands back and looks at Dudley*)

Dudley (*muttering*) Teach you some manners, perhaps.

(Ron *steps forward and turns Dudley's head to face Andrea*)

Claud. Manners, eh? (*He laughs mirthlessly*) Huh, huh! That's likely. (*He turns his head away*)

(Ron *crosses to* c, *picks up the camera and crouches*)

Dudley (*muttering*) Sitting there like a . . .
Ron (*to Claud; interrupting*) You put your arm along the back, will you?

(Claud *puts his left arm along the back of the sofa*)

'S the idea. Look at the lady, though.

(Claud *looks at Andrea*)

(*To Briggs. With pride*) How's that?
Briggs (*crossing to Ron and crouching behind him*) Colossal!
Ron. O.K. then. (*He directs his camera*)
Dudley (*muttering*) Fatuous ass! I'll knock his . . .
Andrea (*sotto voce*) *Will* you be quiet?
Ron. Think of somethin' nice, now.
Briggs (*imploringly*) Please look happy.

(Andrea *resumes her false smile.* Dudley *and* Claud *achieve a tortured travesty of a grin. All are still*)

Ron. Hold it, now. Hold it. (*He flashes the bulb and takes the photograph*)

Dudley ⎫
        ⎬ (*jumping to their feet; together*) ⎰ Right!
Claud ⎭   ⎱ Now then!

(Dudley *and* Claud *make for the french windows.* Ron, *holding his camera protectively above his head, is nearly bowled over in the rush.* Briggs, *in a panic, retreats down* r)

Andrea (*rising*) Don't be so childish, Claud. Dudley!
Claud. I'm sorry, my dear.

(Claud, *taking the cricket bat with him, exits on the sun-deck to* r)

Dudley. He asked for it.

(Dudley *exits on the sun-deck to* r. Ron *begins enthusiastically to follow*)

Andrea (*to Ron*) You come back here.
Ron (*stopping*) Can't I just . . . ? (*He indicates the camera*)
Andrea. No, you can not.

(Ron, *crestfallen, moves down* r)

(*To Briggs*) And don't you dare print any of this, you know.
Briggs. Oh, no, Miss Pigeon, I wouldn't think of . . .

(*The voices of* DUDLEY *and* CLAUD *are heard angrily upraised, off. The others, fascinated, listen*)

DUDLEY (*off*) Now then, you drip!
CLAUD (*off*) Are you prepared to withdraw what you . . . ?
DUDLEY (*off*) I withdraw nothing, you pompous clot.
CLAUD (*off*) Right!
DUDLEY (*off*) You put that . . .

CLAUD ⎫   ⎧ Take your beastly . . . Agh! Ugh! Let
        ⎬   ⎪ go, you . . . Ugh! I'll jolly soon . . .
DUDLEY ⎬ (*off; together*) ⎨ Don't you . . . Oh, you would, would
        ⎪   ⎪ you? All right, I'll knock your . . .
        ⎭   ⎩ Oooh!

(*Grunts, gasps and the sound of blows are heard off. Finally there is a musical, percussive sound, as of a wooden object descending upon a human head, and then silence*)

ANDREA (*scared*) Why has it gone so quiet?

(CLAUD *enters the sun-deck from* R. *His hair is ruffled; his clothes are disordered; there is an abrasion on his cheek-bone and he is out of breath. He carries the cricket bat. He comes into the room and stands up* RC)

CLAUD (*with an air of faint surprise*) Do you know—I think I may have killed him.

CLAUD *takes his handkerchief from his pocket, wipes the end of the bat and moves down* C *as—*

the CURTAIN *falls*

SCENE 2

SCENE—*The same. Thursday afternoon, after lunch.*

When the CURTAIN *rises, the room bears signs of disorder. Newspapers lie about the place and cushions are disarranged. The remains of a scrappy meal for three are still on the table* R. *A large suitcase stands by the kitchen door, and a smaller one, half filled and open, is on the right end of the sofa. Gertrude's bag is on the sun-deck table. The telephone is ringing. There is a short pause, then* ANDREA *enters down the stairs. She wears a simple, tailored dress. Bedroom slippers and disordered hair, however, show that her toilet is not yet complete. She has been crying, and at intervals, she sniffs and gasps spasmodically. She carries a small assortment of underwear, which she hurriedly dumps on the sofa. She then goes to the telephone, lifts the receiver, lays it on the table, takes out a handkerchief, blows her nose, then picks up the receiver.*

Andrea (*into the telephone*) Hullo . . . (*She sniffs*) Oh, Valerie.
You got my message then . . . (*She sniffs and gasps*) What? . . . No,
a touch of hay fever, that's all . . . Well, I get mine in September . . .
(*She sniffs*) What? . . . What phone? . . . This one? . . . No, I don't
think so. But we have been engaged all day. It's hardly stopped
ringing . . . (*She becomes, by degrees, more composed*) Well, newspapers,
mostly . . . Yes, it's this article, dear, in *The Sun* that your little
friend did . . . Oh no, there's nothing wrong with it. She didn't
say anything that—she shouldn't have done. It seems to have
made such a stir, that's all. One can't go out, or anything . . .
Reporters, dear. Scores of them . . . No, only lurking, but there's
one in every bush . . . People? Ordinary ones, you mean? . . .
Darling, you never saw so many people. It's like Derby Day. One
might be living in a car-park—except that they bring their
lunch . . . Well, it depends what you mean by holiday atmosphere,
dear. *They* seem to be enjoying it, but . . . No, quite. And then
there's another thing, Valerie. Mrs O'Connor's gone . . . Without
a word, my dear. Taken her husband and everything . . . I don't
know. I can't imagine what's upset her but, there it is, she's . . .
Yes. So you see, what with one thing and another . . . Well,
Gertrude and I will be leaving as soon as we can, but . . .
What? . . . Oh, no, dear, the house won't be empty . . . Well,
Dudley. (*She becomes a little careful in her manner*) Yes, he's—um—
he's not very well . . . Concussion, dear. He bumped his head . . .
Yes, isn't it, poor pet? So he'll have to be here for a day or so,
anyway—until he can drive himself away—because he's got a
car with him. And Claud will be here, too, to look after him, so . . .
Oh no, he offered to. He's terribly concerned . . . (*She shows signs
of tears. Resentfully*) Well, as a matter of fact, dear, it isn't sweet
of him at all. He ought to be concerned. And, Valerie—it isn't
hay fever, either. It's—it's Claud.

(Claud *enters on the sun-deck from* l. *He is dressed as in the
previous scene. The damage to his face has developed into an angry
bruise. He hurries into the room and begins to cross*)

He's not the man I thought he was, that's all. He's a brute.
He's . . . (*She sees Claud and abruptly changes her tone*) Well, thank
you so much for the house, darling. Be seeing you. Good-bye.
(*She replaces the receiver*)

(Claud *halts up* c. Andrea, *ignoring Claud, moves to the sofa,
sits at the left end, and begins to pack the garments into the suitcase.*
Claud *hovers ingratiatingly*)

Claud (*after a pause*) Been to the chemist. (*He takes a small
bottle from his pocket*) Aspirin. Said he had a headache.
Andrea (*coldly*) Is that surprising?

(*The telephone rings.* Claud *moves to the telephone*)

F

Just say "no", will you?

CLAUD (*lifting the receiver; into the telephone*) No. (*He replaces the receiver*)

ANDREA. And leave the thing off.

(CLAUD *takes the receiver from its cradle and puts it on the table, then comes down* C)

CLAUD (*entreatingly*) Andrea! Can't you forgive me?

ANDREA (*intent on her packing; in apparent surprise*) Forgive you? What for?

CLAUD. Well, for—becoming exasperated with him like that.

ANDREA. If—by "becoming exasperated" you mean nearly beating his brains out—there's nothing to forgive. You can't help having homicidal tendencies, presumably.

CLAUD. But you must believe me. I didn't really mean him any harm. I just happened to have a cricket bat in my hand, that's all.

ANDREA. Some day you may happen to be toying with a meat-axe when you become exasperated.

CLAUD. He hit me. Why aren't you wild with him?

ANDREA. You're supposed to be nicer than he is. There's nothing else to recommend you, you know—if you're not. I don't care what *he* does, anyway. (*She completes the packing, rises and looks around the room*)

CLAUD (*with a flicker of hope*) But you do care what I do?

ANDREA. Not now.

CLAUD. Oh!

ANDREA (*seeing the seaweed on the picture and crossing to it*) I just don't like cosh-boys, that's all. (*She takes down the seaweed, returns to the sofa, sits, carefully folds the seaweed and puts it in the suitcase*)

CLAUD. It's finished, then?

ANDREA. That puts it quite neatly, I think. (*She shuts the case and starts trying to fasten it*)

CLAUD (*humbly*) I see. (*He begins to move slowly* L)

ANDREA. There's no need to go all crushed and silent like that, though.

CLAUD (*stopping and turning*) Why not?

ANDREA (*struggling with the suitcase*) It can't mean all that to you—and it only makes me feel a beast.

CLAUD. Well, I'm sorry, but I happen to *be* crushed and silent.

ANDREA (*kneeling on the suitcase*) That's plain silly, of course. Only yesterday you still weren't sure whether I was fit to be your life partner at all.

CLAUD. I am today, though.

ANDREA (*cynically*) What's convinced you this time?

CLAUD (*moving to* R *of the sofa*) The fact that you can't forgive me, Andrea. You'd like to forgive me. I know you would. But you can't. And any woman who's so morbidly squeamish over a slight act of personal violence like that, couldn't possibly be a killer.

ANDREA (*thoughtfully*) I see. (*She stops fiddling with the suitcase*)

CLAUD. So you needn't feel a beast, or anything. I'm—I'm happy to lose you—that way.

ANDREA (*gently*) Is it so important to you to be able to believe in me, Claud?

CLAUD. It is.

ANDREA (*getting off the suitcase*) Could you do this for me, please?

(CLAUD *moves to the sofa, puts the suitcase on the floor, shuts it, then stands it above the sofa and moves to the sideboard where he pours a drink for himself*)

(*She watches Claud with a worried look*) Well, I'm sorry, Claud, but you must see what a shock it's been. I thought you were the last person to do a thing like that.

CLAUD (*standing with his back to Andrea*) I also thought I was the last person to do a thing like that.

ANDREA (*crossing down L*) Later on, of course, I may feel differently about it.

(CLAUD *turns and looks hopefully at Andrea*)

At the moment, though, I just can't bear the thought of you.

CLAUD. Oh! (*He turns back to the sideboard*)

ANDREA. I've made other plans now, too.

CLAUD. I know. (*He stands with his head bent*)

(ANDREA *stares unhappily at Claud for a moment*)

ANDREA (*moving up L; suddenly*) Well, I wish you wouldn't be so humble and contrite about it. I want to get on.

CLAUD (*turning*) Everything conspires to make me humble and contrite—(*he indicates the staircase*) even he.

ANDREA (*surprised*) Dudley?

CLAUD. Hasn't shown a spark of resentment.

ANDREA. Oh well—as far as that goes—he doesn't know.

CLAUD. Doesn't know what?

ANDREA. That you hit him. He *has* lost his memory this time.

CLAUD (*astonished*) You don't mean it!

ANDREA. And, although you don't deserve it, Claud, I haven't enlightened him, because I don't like an "atmosphere", but . . .

(GERTRUDE *enters down the stairs. She moves briskly down L, then crosses down R, apparently looking for something*)

CLAUD. Do you mean to say . . . ?

(*There is a knock at the front door off*)

ANDREA (*moving to the passage up L*) Oh, bother!

CLAUD. You're not going to answer it, are you?

F*

ANDREA. It can't be a reporter, dear. The police are keeping them out now.

(ANDREA *exits by the passage*)

CLAUD (*putting his drink on the sideboard and crossing to the stairs*) Oh, well, I'll give him his aspirin.

(CLAUD *exits up the stairs.* GERTRUDE *moves up* R, *peers out of the french windows, sees her plastic bag on the table, goes on to the sun-deck, picks up the bag, then comes into the room and moves slowly down* C, *putting on the earphone. Having done this, she switches on, then stops and looks concerned. She switches on and off once or twice, shakes the bag, makes a small cooing noise into it, then abruptly moves to the chair down* R, *sits and draws out the entire electrical contents, a weird, complex and dangling collection of coils, valves, batteries and wires. She dumps the apparatus into her lap and begins to examine it.*

ANDREA *enters slowly by the passage. She is reading the last page of a wad of telegraph forms*)

ANDREA (*moving above the sofa*) Well, of all things. The little beast. Listen to this, darling. It's a telegram—from the Feature Editor of the *Sunday Record*. He says—(*she reads*) "Phoebe Hogg, chief witness for the prosecution at your trial, walked into this office this morning and made us a proposition. Stop. It seems that her evidence was false. Stop. She was in love with your husband and consequently did not like you." (*To Gertrude*) Well, that's only natural, I suppose. (*She reads*) "She was much upset at his demise and wanted to make somebody suffer for it. Stop. You were the obvious choice. Stop. Also handy. Stop. Says accusation was made under influence of gin and tonic. Stop. Later found it awkward to retract. Stop. But claims would not have let you hang." (*To Gertrude*) Well, that's a comfort, anyway. (*She reads*) "She has today read press report of your husband's return also his statement that her testimony was untrue and now confidently awaits prosecution for perjury. Stop. Making hay, she therefore offers to sell us, while still in a position to do so, a one-thousand-word confession under the title: 'My Fight with my Conscience', disclosure being inevitable anyway. Stop. Do you object? Stop. Congratulations. Stop. We do not like Miss Hogg." Now isn't that nice? (*She takes the bottom form from the bunch, puts the remainder on the back of the sofa, then moves to the telephone table*) And the length of it, my dear. Must have cost a fortune. Prepaid answer, too. (*She picks up the pencil and scribbles on the form, reading aloud as she writes*) "Of course I don't object."

(ANDREA *picks up the form and exits with it by the passage up* L. GERTRUDE *completes her examination and replaces the apparatus in the bag*)

(*Off*) Thank you so much.

(Andrea *enters by the passage.* Gertrude *rises and crosses to the stairs*)

(*Moving down behind the sofa*) So that will be out on Sunday. Won't Claud be pleased?

Gertrude. Just as well we are going, dear. I think I've blown a valve.

Andrea (*staring at Gertrude*) Do you mean to tell me . . . ?

(*A sort of grunting groan issues from the stairway off*)

Dudley!

(Dudley *and* Claud *enter down the stairs.* Dudley *wears a dressing-gown over pyjamas, and slippers. There is an impressive dressing on his forehead, and he has a spectacular black eye. He moves with care, for fear of jarring his head. His hair is tousled, and he looks pretty much of a wreck. The state of his temper is deplorable.* Claud *officiously supports him by the arm.* Dudley, *seeing Gertrude, shields his dressing from her*)

Gertrude (*playfully*) Still a late riser, I see.

(Gertrude *exits up the stairs*)

Andrea (*crossing to the armchair down* l) What are you doing down here? (*She picks up the cushion from the chair*)

Dudley (*moving below the sofa; with ill grace*) I'm all right.

Andrea (*turning and putting the cushion on the sofa*) You're not all right. The doctor said . . .

Dudley (*interrupting*) Damn the doctor! Oooh! (*He closes his eyes, frowns with pain and sinks on to the sofa, at the left end*)

Andrea (*swiftly arranging the cushions*) Headache no better?

Dudley (*putting up his feet*) No.

Claud (*moving to* r *of the sofa*) Won't take his aspirin.

Andrea (*standing* l *of the sofa*) Well, I could have told you that, dear.

Claud. Why not, though?

Dudley. I don't like medicine.

Claud (*taking the bottle of aspirin from his pocket*) Well, just this once, old man.

Dudley. No!

Claud. Come on. To please Andrea.

Dudley. *No!* Oooh!

Andrea (*to Claud*) You see?—I'm sorry, but I must get on.

(Andrea *exits up the stairs.* Dudley *closes his eyes*)

Claud (*replacing the aspirins in his pocket*) Would you like another cushion?

Dudley (*grumpily*) No, thank you.

Claud. Cigarette?

DUDLEY. No, thank you.

CLAUD. Good thing you happened to have a bag with you (*he indicates Dudley's dressing-gown*) otherwise it . . .

DUDLEY (*opening his eyes; interrupting loudly*) And I don't feel chatty either.

CLAUD. Oh! (*He crosses to the left end of the window seat, sits, puts on his spectacles and picks up a newspaper from the table* R)

DUDLEY (*not very graciously*) I'm sorry.

CLAUD. 'S all right.

DUDLEY. You're being very good to me. I don't know why, I'm sure.

(CLAUD *looks uncomfortable*)

(*He glares at Claud*) What happened?

CLAUD. Huh?

DUDLEY. What really happened? She told me I fell down.

CLAUD (*uneasily*) You—er—you can't remember, I understand?

DUDLEY. Not a thing.

CLAUD (*feebly*) What makes you think you didn't fall down, then?

DUDLEY. Listen. At four-thirty she says she's going to kill me. At four-forty I'm attacked with a blunt instrument. Doesn't that imply anything?

CLAUD (*rising; horrified*) You don't think *she* did it?

DUDLEY. Do *you* believe I tumbled over?

CLAUD (*replacing the paper on the table and removing his spectacles*) No—to be honest—I . . .

DUDLEY (*interrupting*) Exactly. Well, who else is there with a reputation for trying to do me in?

CLAUD (*crossing to* R *of the sofa*) Well, nobody of course, but that's no reason for assuming . . .

DUDLEY (*interrupting; irritably*) Look! What's the sense in talking like that? *You* know she bashed me as well as I do. I expect you were even there. As a matter of fact, you probably intervened and stopped her.

CLAUD. What?

DUDLEY (*indicating on his own face the position of Claud's injury*) How else did you come by that?

CLAUD. Well, *she* didn't do it, anyway.

DUDLEY (*wearily irascible*) Claud. I know you're the sort of man who remains loyal through thick and thin, and it's frightfully admirable and all that, but don't come it with me this afternoon, there's a good chap—not when I feel like this. (*Suddenly shouting*) It's *not good* for me. Oooh! (*He clutches his head*)

CLAUD (*shrugging*) Very well. (*He moves up* R)

DUDLEY (*after a pause*) Have I got anything to show for it—(*he indicates his dressing*) apart from this?

CLAUD (*turning*) Haven't you seen yourself?

DUDLEY. Not yet. Why?

CLAUD (*with a note of malicious satisfaction*) Oh! Well, I'll get you a mirror. (*He crosses to the stairs*)

(GERTRUDE *and* ANDREA *enter down the stairs.* GERTRUDE *wears her hat and coat, and carries gloves, her plastic bag and the cricket bat.* ANDREA *has also put on her coat as well as shoes and a smart little hat. She carries her slippers and handbag.* CLAUD *stands aside.* ANDREA *moves above the sofa and puts the slippers and handbag on the back of it*)

GERTRUDE (*crossing to the table* R) What a good thing you didn't do it up—(*she holds up the cricket bat*) Mr Merrilees. I needn't send it now. (*She puts the bag on the table and begins to put on her gloves*) I needn't send it now.

ANDREA (*picking up the suitcase above the sofa; to Claud*) Are you going up, dear? (*She takes the suitcase to the passage up* L *and puts it down*)

CLAUD. Yes.

ANDREA. Bring down Gertrude's suitcase, will you? (*She returns to the sofa*)

(CLAUD *nods and exits up the stairs*)

GERTRUDE (*to Andrea*) Perhaps you'd ask him to bring my suitcase down, dear?

ANDREA. I have.

GERTRUDE. Hmm?

ANDREA (*shouting*) I have.

(DUDLEY *winces and closes his eyes.* GERTRUDE *looks perplexed*)

(*To Dudley*) Oh, I'm so sorry. (*She moves to the telephone table, grabs the writing pad and pencil, crosses to Gertrude, scribbles on the pad, and shows it to her*)

GERTRUDE. Oh, you have. Thank you. What's the matter with Dudley, dear?

(ANDREA *puts her finger to her lips*)

(*Whispering*) Isn't he well?

(ANDREA *points to her head*)

(*In a horrified whisper*) Mental?

(ANDREA *glances anxiously at Dudley, scribbles on the pad, and shows it to Gertrude*)

(*Relieved*) Oh—headache. Oh, well. (*She scrabbles in her bag. Whispering*) See if you can get him to take one of my pettacattel powders. (*She takes a paper packet of powder from the bag and hands it to Andrea*) They're the very thing for headache—*and* rheumatism, if he ever gets that. (*Loudly for Dudley's benefit*) Well, I'll just put these things safely in the car, and then I'll come back and say good-bye.

(GERTRUDE *picks up the bat, winks conspiratorially, crosses and exits by the passage up* L)

ANDREA (*considering*) Now, let me see—have I forgotten anything? (*She moves to* R *of the sofa*) Oh yes—a young woman rang up.

DUDLEY (*opening his eyes*) What young woman?

ANDREA. I don't know, dear, but she'd seen the papers and . . .

DUDLEY (*interrupting*) Didn't she give a name?

ANDREA. No. She sounded awfully pretty, though, and quite well off. One could always *get* the name, of course, through the registration number—if necessary. I have made a note of it.

DUDLEY (*lifting his head; irritably*) What are you talking about? What registration number?

ANDREA. Of her car, Dudley. Didn't I say? The one you've got. She wanted to know what you'd done with it. Said you hadn't been home since Monday.

DUDLEY (*deflating*) Oh!

ANDREA. I told her you hadn't sold it or anything—was that right?

DUDLEY (*anxiously*) Was she cross?

ANDREA (*as if reluctant to say it*) She was, rather.

DUDLEY. About the car, you mean?

ANDREA. That, and the fact that she hadn't realized you were married until she read this morning's paper.

DUDLEY (*avoiding Andrea's eye*) Oh!

ANDREA. Also, apparently, you went off and left the bath water running. It's too bad of you, really.

(DUDLEY *has no comment to make*)

(*She moves to the telephone table and replaces the pad and pencil*) Now is there anything I can get you before we go?

DUDLEY. I shouldn't mind a drink.

ANDREA. Of course. (*She moves to the sideboard*) There is one here already. Is that Claud's?

DUDLEY. I suppose so.

(CLAUD *enters down the stairs. He carries Gertrude's suitcase and a shaving mirror.* ANDREA *pours a drink for Dudley.* CLAUD *puts the suitcase on the floor at the foot of the stairs, then moves to* L *of the sofa*)

CLAUD (*handing the mirror to Dudley*) I'm sorry. I had to look for one. (*He returns up* L)

(DUDLEY *sits up facing out front and looks at his face in the mirror*)

DUDLEY. Good heavens! (*He stares in horror*)

(CLAUD *picks up Gertrude's suitcase*)

ANDREA (*to Claud*) Can you manage the other one, too, dear?

(CLAUD *nods, picks up the suitcase in the passage, and exits by the passage up* L)

DUDLEY (*angrily*) Why didn't someone tell me about this? I shan't be able to go out for weeks.

(ANDREA *turns with the drink on one hand and the powder still absently clutched in the other*)

ANDREA. Well, never mind, dear. Claud will be . . . (*She breaks off, looks first at the powder, then at the drink and, becoming slightly furtive in manner, returns to the sideboard*) Claud will be able to—(*she puts the glass on the sideboard and unfolds the packet of powder*) stay with you. (*She empties the powder into the glass*)

(*Seeing this in his mirror*, DUDLEY *starts, stares for a moment in fascinated horror, then, rising slowly, he moves away* R)

(*She swishes the glass*) He had arranged to take a couple of weeks off, remember. (*She turns and moves to* R *of the coffee table*) Should you be on your feet, dear?

DUDLEY. Evidently not.

ANDREA (*putting the glass on the coffee table*) Well—you drink this. (*She crosses to* L *of the sofa*)

DUDLEY. *Thank* you.

ANDREA. Now—is there anything else you'll need?

DUDLEY (*pointing at the drink*) Not if I drink that, anyway. (*He puts the mirror on the table* R)

ANDREA (*puzzled*) What do you mean, dear?

DUDLEY. What do you do it for, Andrea—fun?

ANDREA. Do what?

DUDLEY. Put things in my whisky.

ANDREA. Oh! (*She moves above the sofa*)

DUDLEY (*crossing to* R *of the sofa*) You know you can get rid of me now—without that—legitimately—any time you like. You've only got to trace the woman through her number-plates and you've got all the evidence you want. What's the idea?

ANDREA. That may be perfectly platonic, for all I know.

DUDLEY (*fiercely*) Well, it isn't—see?

ANDREA. Oh!

DUDLEY. I'll *give* the name and address if you like.

ANDREA. You will?

DUDLEY (*crossing to* R; *waving his arms*) You can have a selection of names and addresses. (*He sits on the left end of the window seat*)

ANDREA. Well, thank you, Dudley. That is kind.

DUDLEY. Don't mention it.

ANDREA. I've no particular need of a divorce any more—as it happens.

(CLAUD *enters by the passage and wanders disconsolately down* L)

DUDLEY (*surprised*) You haven't?

ANDREA (*glancing at Claud*) It may come in useful, though—some time.

(*There is a slight pause.* ANDREA *begins to look distressed*)

CLAUD (*dismally*) Anything else to go?

ANDREA. I don't think so. What's Gertrude doing?

CLAUD. Waiting for you apparently. She's sitting in the car.

ANDREA. Oh! (*She picks up her handbag and slippers, then hesitates, looking wretched*) That's all, then, isn't it? (*She looks from one to the other*)

(CLAUD *nods faintly.* DUDLEY *turns his head away*)

(*She replaces the bag and slippers on the back of the sofa and crosses to Dudley. Sadly*) Well—good-bye, Dudley darling. (*She lays a hand on his shoulder*)

(DUDLEY *cringes*)

I do hope we shall never meet again. (*She turns and crosses to Claud. Emotionally*) Dear—dear Claud.

CLAUD (*fighting his own emotion*) I'll see you off. (*He takes a step towards the passage*)

ANDREA. No—I'd rather you didn't.

CLAUD (*gruffly*) Good-bye, then.

ANDREA (*her voice trembling*) You will keep in touch, though, won't you—in case I get over it. I do hope I do. (*She kisses him lightly on the cheek*) It would be such a pity. (*She goes to the sofa, picks up her bag and slippers and moves on to the passage*)

CLAUD. But where are you going?

ANDREA (*surprised*) To Gertrude's, dear.

CLAUD. I know, but after that? I must have an address.

ANDREA. Oh, but I shall be living with Gertrude. Didn't you realize?

CLAUD. No. Indefinitely?

ANDREA. Well, that's the present arrangement. I wanted to see that she ends her days in peace.

CLAUD. Oh!

ANDREA. But that's only if I've nothing else to do, Claud. (*Miserably*) Good-bye.

CLAUD (*murmuring*) Good-bye.

(ANDREA *exits by the passage up* L. CLAUD *moves to* L *of the coffee table, picks up Dudley's glass, and drinks.* DUDLEY, *wearing a puzzled and uneasy look, seems absorbed in some half-formed doubt of his own*)

DUDLEY (*half to himself*) She "wanted to see that she ends her days in . . ." (*He is suddenly galvanized with horror*) No! (*He jumps to his feet*) No!

CLAUD (*startled*) What's the matter?

(GERTRUDE *enters by the passage*)

DUDLEY. Don't you see what she's up to? It's going to be Aunt Maggie all over again.

GERTRUDE (*moving down* C; *to Claud*) I'm so sorry, I forgot to say good-bye. (*She holds out her hand*)

CLAUD (*crossing to* L *of Gertrude; to Dudley*) What are you talking about? (*He takes Gertrude's hand*) You said good-bye to me outside.

GERTRUDE ⎫
DUDLEY ⎬ (*together*) ⎧ I'm so glad to have met you, Mr Merrilees.
(*Crossing to* R *of Gertrude*) She's after her money, you fool.

CLAUD (*smiling courteously*) Good-bye, Miss Pigeon.

(GERTRUDE *turns to* DUDLEY *who seizes both her hands*)

DUDLEY (*shouting*) Don't go with her, Gertrude.

GERTRUDE. It's been so nice having you alive again, Dudley.

DUDLEY. Gertrude—I im*plore* you.

GERTRUDE. It's no good trying to start a conversation with me now, dear. (*She proffers her cheek for Dudley to kiss*)

DUDLEY. But, listen . . .

GERTRUDE. Aren't you going to kiss me?

DUDLEY (*pecking her frantically*) She's going to *mur*der you.

GERTRUDE (*with satisfaction*) *That's* right. (*She turns and bustles up* L)

DUDLEY (*following Gertrude and clutching at her arm*) Gertrude!

GERTRUDE. Write to me, dear—if it's important.

(GERTRUDE *exits by the passage up* L)

DUDLEY (*turning*) What are we to do?

CLAUD (*sitting on the sofa*) If you ask me—you're hysterical.

DUDLEY (*moving down* C) But the woman's a murderess.

CLAUD. Nonsense! (*He drains the glass*)

DUDLEY. You must be half insane, you know. First she shoves me in the sea—then she slugs me—then she tries to poison me—and you sit there and . . .

CLAUD (*interrupting*) What makes you think she's tried to poison you, for heaven's sake?

DUDLEY. Because I *saw* her.

CLAUD. Saw her?

DUDLEY. Not five minutes ago. Put it in my whisky. *Brought* it to me. (*Thumping the coffee table to emphasize each word*) *Stood* it down there——

(CLAUD *starts slightly, looks at his empty glass and sits up*)

—and waited for me to drink it.

CLAUD (*a disquieting thought rapidly developing*) Stood it down there?

(DUDLEY *moves to the sideboard, picks up the powder paper and flourishes it at Claud*)

(*In growing alarm*) I say.

DUDLEY. Yes?

CLAUD. Is there another drink up there?

(DUDLEY *is masking Claud's view of the sideboard*)

DUDLEY (*moving* R) Oh, for pity's sake, what does it matter?

CLAUD (*almost with a scream*) There *is*! (*With quivering lips and staring eyes, he puts his glass on the coffee table*)

(ANDREA *enters by the passage*)

ANDREA (*as she enters*) Forgot my suitcase. (*She picks up the remaining suitcase*)

DUDLEY (*with a step towards Andrea; portentously*) Andrea!

(ANDREA *catches sight of the stricken Claud, puts the suitcase down again and goes to him, ignoring Dudley.* DUDLEY *crosses and stands above Andrea*)

ANDREA. Don't take it so hard, darling. Just give me a week or so, and I'm sure it'll be all right.

DUDLEY. If you take that poor old girl away from here—if you so much as go out through that door—so help me, I'll get the police.

ANDREA (*picking up the bunch of telegraph forms and thrusting them into Claud's hand*) Here! This'll cheer you. (*She moves up* L)

(CLAUD, *sunk in his growing terror, seems hardly to notice. Breathing hard, he flings the forms from him and begins to undo his collar and tie*)

DUDLEY (*moving to Andrea*) Andrea!

ANDREA (*picking up the suitcase*) I'm afraid I can't stop now to find out what you're talking about, Dudley, but it sounds to me as if you're going to make yourself look awfully silly over something, dear.

(ANDREA *exits by the passage up* L)

DUDLEY (*following to the passage and shouting after her*) I warn you, Andrea. I mean it. (*He turns*) Right! (*He strides to the telephone, lifts the receiver and shouts into it*) Hullo! *Hullo!*

CLAUD (*rising and staggering up* C *to the sideboard; yelling*) For God's sake, man . . .

DUDLEY (*to Claud*) What's the matter with you? (*Into the telephone*) Get me the police.

CLAUD (*half collapsing over the sideboard*) Don't fiddle with the police, you fool. Get a *doctor.*

DUDLEY (*bellowing into the telephone*) Hullo! *Hullo!*

CURTAIN

FURNITURE AND PROPERTY PLOT

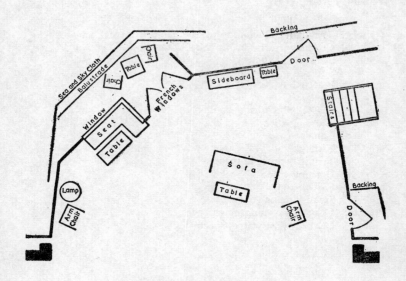

ACT I

On stage: Built-in window seat. *On it:* cushions

Low dining table. *On it:* 2 side plates, 1 large table mat, 2
small table mats, 2 napkins, 2 wine glasses, 2 coffee cups
and saucers, 2 coffee spoons, cruet, empty wine bottle

Sideboard. *On it:* table lamp, bowl of flowers, tray with bottle
of whisky, syphon of soda, 4 glasses

Occasional table. *On it:* table lamp, telephone, writing-pad,
pencil

2 armchairs. *On them:* cushions

Low rectangular coffee table. *On it:* box with cigarettes, ashtray, magazines, Andrea's handbag, bridal bouquet

Standard lamp

Picture on wall L

Picture on wall up ɑ

Sofa. *On it:* cushions

Mirror on wall down R

Carpet on floor
Rug under sofa
Window curtains
On sun-deck: outdoor table, 2 outdoor chairs
Lamps lit
French windows open
Window curtains open

Off stage: Tray (MRS O'CONNOR)
Crumb tray and brush (MRS O'CONNOR)
Seaweed (ANDREA)
Suitcase
Bowler hat
Overcoat
Bag of golf clubs
Shooting-stick
Camera-case
Kitbag
Tennis racquet in press
Dressing-case
Fishing-rod
Small suitcase
Personal: DUDLEY: evening newspaper
CLAUD: wrist watch, spectacles

ACT II

Strike: Newspaper, handbag, overcoat, bag of golf clubs, shooting-stick, camera-case, kitbag, tennis racquet, dressing-case, fishing-rod, small suitcase, dirty glasses
Move flowers from table R to sideboard

Set: *On sideboard:* 4 clean glasses
In sideboard cupboard: 1 large and 3 small mats, 3 small knives, 3 large knives, 3 large forks, cruet
On table R: 2 wine glasses, 3 napkins, bread basket with rolls, vinegar and oil bottles, dish of olives, 2 side plates
Under cushion on sofa: Andrea's handkerchief
On coffee table: American magazine on top of pile
Lamps out
French windows open
Window curtains open
Kitchen door up L open

Off stage: Bowler hat, umbrella, brief-case. *In it:* documents (CLAUD)
    2 suitcases (DUDLEY)
    Claud's raincoat (DUDLEY)
    Black plastic carrier bag. *In it:* hearing aid, writing-pad, foun-
        tain pen, envelopes, small papers of powder (GERTRUDE)
    Cricket bat (GERTRUDE)
    Tray. *On it:* side plate, wine glass (MRS O'CONNOR)
    Golf clubs
    Shooting-stick
    Camera-case
    Kitbag
    Tennis racquet
    Dressing-case
    Fishing-rod
    Small suitcase

Personal: CLAUD: spectacles

ACT III

SCENE I

Strike: Dinner things from table R, golf clubs, shooting-stick, suitcase,
    camera-case, kitbag, tennis racquet, dressing-case, fishing-
    rod, small suitcase, dirty glasses
Move flowers from sideboard to table R
Set: *On sideboard:* 4 clean glasses
    Under cushion on chair down L: novel
    On coffee table: woman's magazine on top of pile
    On sun-deck table: tray. *On it:* 2 cups, 2 saucers, 2 teaspoons, sugar
        basin, teapot, milk jug, tea cosy, muffin dish, tea cloth
    On back of sun-deck chair: bathing costume, towel
Lamps out
French windows open
Window curtains open
Kitchen door open

Off stage: Satchel. *In it:* notebook, pencil (BRIGGS)
    Press camera with flash-bulb attachment (RON)
    Leather plate carrier (RON)
    Bag with hearing aid. *In it:* writing-pad, fountain pen, stamped
        envelope (GERTRUDE)
    Time-table (ANDREA)
    Copy of *The Times*, bowler hat, umbrella, brief-case. *In it:*
        thick sheaf of papers (CLAUD)

Personal: RON: chewing gum
            CLAUD: spectacles, handkerchief
            ANDREA: handkerchief

SCENE 2

Strike: Legal papers from floor, novel, legal paper and brief-case from
          coffee table, umbrella from sideboard, bowler hat, newspaper
          from table R, tea things from sun-deck table, bathing costume,
          towel from sun-deck chair, dirty glasses, cricket bat
Move flowers from table R to sideboard
Disorder magazines on coffee table
Disorder cushions

Set: *On sideboard:* 4 clean glasses
       On table R: 3 plates, 3 knives, cups and saucers, spoons, plate with
          lettuce leaf, piece of cheese, orange, butter dish, loaf and bread-
          knife on bread board, newspaper
       On sofa (at R *end):* small suitcase, open. *In it:* clothing
       Up L: large suitcase
       On armchair down L: magazine
       On floor down L: open newspaper
       On sun-deck table: Gertrude's bag with hearing aid. *In it:* white paper
          containing brown powder
Lamps out
French windows open
Window curtains open

Off stage: 8 sheet telegram (ANDREA)
             4 pieces of lady's underwear (ANDREA)
             Cricket bat (GERTRUDE)
             Shaving mirror (CLAUD)
             Gertrude's suitcase (CLAUD)
             Handbag (ANDREA)
             Slippers (ANDREA)

Personal: ANDREA: handkerchief
            CLAUD: bottle of aspirins, spectacles

LIGHTING PLOT

Fittings required: standard lamp (practical)
                   2 table lamps (practical)

Interior. Same scene throughout
    THE MAIN ACTING AREAS are R, RC, C, LC and up L
    THE APPARENT SOURCES OF LIGHT are, in daytime, large windows
          up R, and at night, a standard lamp down R with table lamps
          up C and up L

ACT I A September evening
To open Dusk outside window
        Stand and table lamps lit
No cues

ACT II Early evening
To open Daylight outside window
        Standard and table lamps out
        Effect of setting sun
Cue 1 GERTRUDE enters   (Page 43)
        Commence slow dim of lights for setting sun, effect
          to continue until end of Act

ACT III, SCENE 1 Afternoon
To open Brilliant sunlight
No cues

ACT III, SCENE 2 Afternoon
To open Sunlight
No cues

MUSIC PLOT

ACT I

Cue 1   Before rise of CURTAIN   (Page 1)
           Trial and Error Theme
           Fade as CURTAIN rises

Cue 2   MRS O'CONNOR enters   (Page 1)
           Radio music, *'Tis Only a Tear* and *My Fireside Heaven*
           Switch off as MRS O'CONNOR exits and closes door   (Page 4)

Cue 3   MRS O'CONNOR enters   (Page 14)
           Radio music, *My Gipsy Heart*
           Switch off as MRS O'CONNOR exits and closes door   (Page 14)

ACT II

Cue 4   Before rise of CURTAIN
           Trial and Error Theme   (Page 31)
           Fade as CURTAIN rises

Cue 5   As CURTAIN rises   (Page 31)
           Radio music, *Olympus March*
           Switch off as MRS O'CONNOR closes door   (Page 31)

Cue 6   MRS O'CONNOR opens door   (Page 31)
           Radio music, *Prepare for Action*
           Switch off as MRS O'CONNOR closes door   (Page 32)

Cue 7   MRS O'CONNOR exits   (Page 32)
           Brief burst of radio music, *Entry of the Gladiators*, as
               door opens and shuts

ACT III

SCENE 1

Cue 8   Before rise of CURTAIN   (Page 53)
           Trial and Error Theme
           Fade as CURTAIN rises

Cue 9 As Curtain rises (Page 53)
Radio music, *Processional*
Switch off as Andrea closes door (Page 53)

Cue 10 Andrea opens door (Page 53)
Radio music, *Processionat*
Andrea: ". . . what time the . . . ? (Page 53)
Switch off music

Cue 11 Andrea: "Thank you so much" (Page 53)
Radio music, *Processional*
Switch off as Mrs O'Connor closes door (Page 54)

Cue 12 Mrs O'Connor exits (Page 55)
Brief burst of radio music, *Processional*, as door opens
   and shuts

Cue 13 Mrs O'Connor enters (Page 66)
Brief burst of radio music, *Processional*, as door opens
   and closes

Cue 14 Mrs O'Connor exits (Page 67)
Brief burst of radio music, *Processional*, as door opens
   and closes

Cue 15 During Scene change (Page 76)
Trial and Error Theme (long version)

SCENE 2

Cue 16 As the Curtain rises (Page 76)
Fade music

RECORDINGS USED

'Tis Only a Tear
My Fireside Heaven } Dance band recording

Processional
Olympus March } Paxton
Prepare for Action

Entry of the Gladiators, Columbia

The theme tune, *Trial and Error*, by Eric Spears, is published by the David Toff Music Publishing Co.